M. Jean Keller, EdD, CTRS
Editor

Caregiving–
Leisure and Aging

*Pre-publication
REVIEWS,
COMMENTARIES,
EVALUATIONS . . .*

"**A** must read for gerontology professionals and educators in the aging network. . . . Compelling and challenging . . . sets the stage for serious consideration of recreation and leisure as an effective intervention/support for caregivers of older adults. . . . Outlines the costs and benefits of leisure and recreation interventions for caregivers and their families."

Jessyna M. McDonald, PhD
*Associate Professor of Parks,
Recreation, and Tourism
Management
Clemson University
Clemson, South Carolina*

Caregiving–
Leisure and Aging

Caregiving–Leisure and Aging has been co-published simultaneously as *Activities, Adaptation & Aging,* Volume 24, Number 2 1999.

The *Activities, Adaptation & Aging*™ Monographic "Separates"

Below is a list of "separates," which in serials librarianship means a special issue simultaneously published as a special journal issue or double-issue *and* as a "separate" hardbound monograph. (This is a format which we also call a "DocuSerial.")

"Separates" are published because specialized libraries or professionals may wish to purchase a specific thematic issue by itself in a format which can be separately cataloged and shelved, as opposed to purchasing the journal on an on-going basis. Faculty members may also more easily consider a "separate" for classroom adoption.

"Separates" are carefully classified separately with the major book jobbers so that the journal tie-in can be noted on new book order slips to avoid duplicate purchasing.

You may wish to visit Haworth's website at . . .

http://www.haworthpressinc.com

. . . to search our online catalog for complete tables of contents of these separates and related publications.

You may also call 1-800-HAWORTH (outside US/Canada: 607-722-5857), or Fax 1-800-895-0582 (outside US/Canada: 607-771-0012), or e-mail at:

getinfo@haworthpressinc.com

Caregiving–Leisure and Aging, edited by M. Jean Keller, EdD, CTRS (Vol. 24, No. 2, 1999). *"A must read for gerontology professionals and educators in the aging network. . . . compelling and challenging. . . . Sets the stage for serious consideration of reaction and leisure as an effective intervention/support for caregivers of older adults. . . . Outlines the costs and benefits of leisure and recreation interventions for caregivers and their families." (Jessyna M. McDonald, PhD, Associate Professor of Parks, Recreation, and Tourism Management, Clemson University, Clemson, South Carolina)*

Preparing Participants for Intergenerational Interaction: Training for Success, edited by Melissa O. Hawkins, MS, Kenneth F. Backman, PhD, and Francis A. McGuire, PhD (Vol. 23, No. 1/2/3, 1998). *"A user-friendly training regimen appropriate to those beginning or seeking to improve intergenerational programs." (Ted Tedrick, PhD, Professor, Sport Management and Leisure Studies, Temple University, Philadelphia, Pennsylvania)*

Horticultural Therapy and the Older Adult Population, edited by Suzanne E. Wells, MS (Vol. 22, No. 1/2/3, 1997). *"Gives a place to find inspiration and ideas for improving care to the elderly through horticultural therapy." (Weed Technology)*

Older Adults with Developmental Disabilities and Leisure: Issues, Policy and Practice, edited by Ted Tedrick, PhD (Vol. 21, No. 3, 1996). *"Offers guidelines for establishing fitness programs and incorporating exercise, arts, and other activities into existing programs for older people with developmental disabilities." (Australian Journal of Ageing)*

The Abusive Elder: Service Considerations, edited by Vera R. Jackson, DSW, ACSW (Vol. 21, No. 1, 1996). *"Recommended for all practitioners who are responsible for institutional care of elderly patients and residents." (Clinical Gerontologist)*

Exercise Programing for Older Adults, edited by Janie Clark, MA (Vol. 20, No. 3, 1996). *"A resource health care providers and exercise program directors will find useful. . . . A good resource for anyone in the health care field and for other professionals who have contact with an older population." (Science Books & Films)*

Volunteerism in Geriatric Settings, edited by Vera R. Jackson, DSW, ACSW (Vol. 20, No. 1, 1996). *"An instructional tool for activity directors and others interested in successful volunteer program management. . . . Provides many insights and ideas for volunteer managers." (Aging Network News)*

Aging Families and Use of Proverbs for Values Enrichment, edited by Vera R. Jackson, DSW, ACSW (Vol. 19, No. 2, 1995). *"A definite asset to those who work with elderly population. . . . Takes a multidimensional perspective and offers the reader a comprehensive look at family and cultural values as they influence the lives of older persons."* (*Jocelyn Turner-Musa, PhD, Assistant Research Professor, Department of Psychiatry, The George Washington University*)

Ethics and Values in Long Term Health Care, edited by Patricia J. Villani, PhD, MPA (Vol. 18, No. 3/4, 1994). *"An effective tool to help staff explore fully the many ethical issues with which they deal and to effectively assist clients and caregivers in making difficult decisions."* (*The Journal of Long-Term Care Administration*)

Therapeutic Humor with the Elderly, Francis A. McGuire, PhD, Rosangela K. Boyd, PhD, and Ann James, PhD (Vol. 17, No. 1, 1993). *"A very intriguing work that is a valuable resource for humor practitioners in all areas of service and programming. It is essential reading for long-term care programmers."* (*Educational Gerontology*)

Story Writing in a Nursing Home: A Patchwork of Memories, edited by Martha Tyler John, PhD (Vol. 16, No. 1, 1992). *"Chock-full of ideas for mental stimulaton and reminiscence. We highly recommend this book for activity professionals in any type of facility who want to develop new or expand upon existing programs."* (*Creative Forecasting*)

Activities in Action: Proceedings of the National Association of Activity Professionals 1990 Conference, edited by Phyllis M. Foster, ACC (Vol. 15, No. 4, 1991). *"An excellent resource for educators, consultants, allied health care professions, providers, regulators, and most of all for those activity professionals unaware of the proud heritage we are the beneficiaries of as NAAP members."* (*Joan M. Flannigan, ACC Quality Assurance Program Coordinator, Care Enterprises, San Diego, California*)

Activities with Developmentally Disabled Elderly and Older Adults, edited by M. Jean Keller, EdD, CTRS (Vol. 15, No. 1/2, 1991). *"A worthwhile addition to the professional library of persons involved in the field of developmental disabilities."* (*International Journal of Disability Development and Education*)

Creative Arts with Older People, edited by Janice McMurray, MSW (Vol. 14, No. 1/2, 1990). *"A compendium 'how to paint a rainbow for those who have never painted with water colors' and suchlike tips, making the point simply and without elaboration."* (*Age and Aging*)

From Deep Within: Poetry Workshops in Nursing Homes, edited by Carol F. Peck, MA (Vol. 13, No. 3, 1989). *"Ms. Peck's ten years experience with such groups provides a deep reservoir from which she draws wisdom and practical skills."* (*Sharon D. Ewing, MFA, "The Poetry Lady" Iliff Nursing Home, Alexandria, Virginia; Creative Writing Teacher, Hollin Hall Senior Center and George Mason University*)

The "Feeling Great!" Wellness Program for Older Adults, Julie C. Weiss, EdD, ATR, LPC (Vol. 12, No. 3/4, 1988). *"A good reference for those who are interested in creating and operating a comprehensive wellness program for the older adult."* (*New York State Journal of Medicine*)

Geragogy: A Theory for Teaching the Elderly, Martha Tyler John, EdD, (Vol. 11, No. 3/4, 1998). *"A handy little book which I plan to use again and again. . ."* (*Journal of Religious Gerontology*)

Adult Day Care: A Practical Guidebook and Manual, Lenore A. Tate, PhD, and Cynthia M. Brennan, MS (Vol. 11, No. 2, 1988). *A valuable guidebook that encourages the promotion and enhancement of adult day care as an essential link in long-term care.*

The Human Factor in Nursing Home Care, David B. Oliver, PhD, and Sally Tureman, MAT (Vol. 10, No. 3/4, 1988). *"Powerfully written and thought-provoking, and would make excellent reading for a variety of groups, including pastors, educators, and those preparing for ministry to the elderly in institutions on either a professional or volunteer basis."* (*Journal of Religious Gerontology*)

"You Bring Out the Music in Me": Music in Nursing Homes, edited by Beckie Karras, RMT-BC, ACC (Vol. 10, No. 1/2, 1988). *"The book illuminates the effective use of music in the lives of people who are suffering age-disabled or terminal illness. . . . The book is an antidote to horror stories we see and read about daily."* (*Stress Medicine*)

Waiting at the Gate: Creativity and Hope in the Nursing Home, Susan Sandel, PhD, ADTR, and David Read Johnson, PhD, RDT (Vol. 9, No. 3, 1987). *"Presents a practical approach to the use of expressive therapies which can be readily applied in a variety of settings."* (*Journal of Long-Term Care Administration*)

Handbook of Group Activities for Impaired Adults, Elsbeth Martindale, PsyD, and Scott Cabot Willis, PhD (Vol. 9, No. 2, 1987). *"Excellent ideas for activities for staff working in long term care facilities, day hospitals and day care, or nursing homes."* (Physiotherapy Canada)

Therapeutic Activities with the Impaired Elderly, edited by Phyllis M. Foster, ACC (Vol. 8, No. 3/4, 1986). *"Full of ideas and examples for creative programming with groups of elderly people."* (Journal of the Physical Therapy Association)

Computer Technology and the Aged: Implications and Applications for Activity Programs, edited by Francis A. McGuire, PhD (Vol. 8, No. 1, 1986). *"An excellent resource for those working with the elderly."* (Physiotherapy Canada)

What Do I Do?: How to Care for, Comfort, and Commune with Your Nursing Home Elder, Revised and Illustrated Edition, Katherine L. Karr, MEd (Vol. 7, No. 1, 1985). *"Practical . . . suggests specific actions that will improve the physical, emotional, mental, and spiritual well-being of a resident . . . Generously illustrated with sensitive photographs."* (Change)

Innovations in Activities for the Elderly. Proceedings of the National Association of Activity Professionals Convention, edited by Jane D. Cook (Vol. 6, No. 3/4, 1985). *"Easy to read. . . . Practical "how to" information available to the front-line worker and the portrayal of a sense of dynamism in working with an elderly population."* (Canadian Journal of Occupational Therapy)

Writers Have No Age: Creative Writing with Older Adults, Leonore M. Coberly, MBA, Jeri McCormick, and Karen Updike (Vol. 6, No. 2, 1985). *"Highly recommended for the adult educator or anyone who is interested in both writing and older adults."* (Educational Gerontology)

Educational Activity Programs for Older Adults: A 12-Month Idea Guide for Adult Education Instructors and Activity Directors in Gerontology, Janice Lake Williams, BA, and Janet Downs, MA (Vol. 5, No. 3/4, 1984). *"An enthusiastic and caring work which provides a wealth of ideas for use in rehabilitation programmes for the elderly."* (British Journal of Occupational Therapy)

Expressive Therapy with Elders and the Disabled: Touching the Heart of Life, Jules C. Weiss, EdD, LPC, ATR (Vol. 5, No. 1/2, 1984). *"This powerful guide aids service providers in becoming more aware of the sensitivity and understanding required to reach many who are often considered unreachable."* (The Gerontologist)

Pets and the Elderly: The Therapeutic Bond, Odean Cusack, BA, and Elaine Smith, BA (Vol. 4, No. 2/3, 1984). *"An in-depth look at the benefits of pet therapy not only for institutions, but also for aged residents."* (Journal of Applied Rehabilitation Counseling)

Activities and the "Well Elderly", edited by Phyllis Foster, ACC (Vol. 3, No. 2, 1983). *Authoritative insights into activities work with noninstitutionalized "well" elderly.*

Drama Activities with Older Adults: A Handbook for Leaders, Anne H. Thurman, MA, and Carol Ann Piggins, BS (Vol. 2, No. 2/3, 1982). *"Well-organized, it lays an excellent foundation upon which to build quality drama activities that will add new dimensions to most older adult programs."* (The Gerontologist)

Caregiving–Leisure and Aging

M. Jean Keller, EdD, CTRS
Editor

Caregiving–Leisure and Aging has been co-published simultaneously as *Activities, Adaptation & Aging,* Volume 24, Number 2 1999.

The Haworth Press, Inc.
New York • London • Oxford

Caregiving–Leisure and Aging has been co-published simultaneously as *Activities, Adaptation & Aging,* Volume 24, Number 2 1999.

Library of Congress Cataloging-in-Publication Data

Caregiving–leisure and aging / M. Jean Keller, editor.
      p. cm.
      "Has been co-published simultaneously as Activities, adaptation & aging, volume 24, number 2 1999."
      Includes bibliographical references and index.
      ISBN 0-7890-0776-2 (alk. paper)–ISBN 0-7890-0799-1 (alk. paper)
      1. Aged–Home care–Psychological aspects. 2. Caregivers–Recreation. 3. Leisure. I Keller, M. Jean.
HV1451.C327 1999
362.6–dc21
                                   99-051926
                                      CIP

INDEXING & ABSTRACTING

Contributions to this publication are selectively indexed or abstracted in print, electronic, online, or CD-ROM version(s) of the reference tools and information services listed below. This list is current as of the copyright date of this publication. See the end of this section for additional notes.

- *Abstracts in Social Gerontology: Current Literature on Aging*

- *Abstracts of Research in Pastoral Care & Counseling*

- *AgeInfo CD-ROM*

- *AgeLine Database*

- *Alzheimer's Disease Education & Referral Center (ADEAR)*

- *Brown University Geriatric Research Application Digest "Abstracts Section"*

- *BUBL Information Service. An Internet-based Information Service for the UK higher education community<URL:http://bubl.ac.uk/>*

- *Cambridge Scientific Abstracts*

- *CINAHL (Cumulative Index to Nursing & Allied Health Literature), in print, also on CD-ROM from CD PLUS, EBSCO, and SilverPlatter, and online from CDP Online (formerly BRS), Data-Star, and PaperChase. (Support materials include Subject Heading List, Database Search Guide, and instructional video.)*

- *CNPIEC Reference Guide: Chinese National Directory of Foreign Periodicals*

- *Combined Health Information Database (CHID)*

- *Family Studies Database (online and CD/ROM)*

- *Health Care Literature Information Network/HECLINET*

- *Human Resources Abstracts (HRA)*

(continued)

- *IBZ International Bibliography of Periodical Literature*

- *Leisure, Recreation and Tourism Abstracts, c/o CAB International/CAB ACCESS . . . available in print, diskettes updated weekly, and on INTERNET. Providing full bibliographic listings, author affiliation, augmented keyword searching*

- *Mental Health Abstracts (online through DIALOG)*

- *National Clearinghouse for Primary Care Information (NCPCI)*

- *REHABDATA, National Rehabilitation Information Center. Searches are available in large-print, cassette or Braille format and all are available on PC-compatible diskette. Also accessible via the Internet at http//www.naric.com/naric.*

- *New Literature on Old Age*

- *OT BibSys*

- *Psychological Abstracts (PsycINFO)*

- *Referativnyi Zhurnal (Abstracts Journal of the All-Russian Institute of Scientific and Technical Information)*

- *Social Planning/Policy & Development Abstracts (SOPODA)*

- *Social Work Abstracts*

- *Sociological Abstracts (SA)*

- *Special Educational Needs Abstracts*

- *Sport Search*

- *Studies on Women Abstracts*

(continued)

Special Bibliographic Notes related to special journal issues (separates) and indexing/abstracting:

- indexing/abstracting services in this list will also cover material in any "separate" that is co-published simultaneously with Haworth's special thematic journal issue or DocuSerial. Indexing/abstracting usually covers material at the article/chapter level.
- monographic co-editions are intended for either non-subscribers or libraries which intend to purchase a second copy for their circulating collections.
- monographic co-editions are reported to all jobbers/wholesalers/approval plans. The source journal is listed as the "series" to assist the prevention of duplicate purchasing in the same manner utilized for books-in-series.
- to facilitate user/access services all indexing/abstracting services are encouraged to utilize the co-indexing entry note indicated at the bottom of the first page of each article/chapter/contribution.
- this is intended to assist a library user of any reference tool (whether print, electronic, online, or CD-ROM) to locate the monographic version if the library has purchased this version but not a subscription to the source journal.
- individual articles/chapters in any Haworth publication are also available through the Haworth Document Delivery Service (HDDS).

Caregiving–
Leisure and Aging

CONTENTS

ABOUT THE EDITOR

M. Jean Keller, EdD, CTRS, is Dean of the College of Education and Professor of Recreation and Leisure Studies at the University of North Texas. She has written or edited ten books and ten refereed chapters, and authored over one hundred articles on therapeutic recreation and gerontological topics. In addition, she has given 300 presentations in the United States and several countries. She is the recipient of national, regional, and statewide awards including the Distinguished Professional Award presented by the National Therapeutic Recreation Society. She has served on the Board of Directors for the National Council for Therapeutic Recreation Certification; as Program Coordinator for the Gerontological Society of America; and as Chair of the Therapeutic Recreation Symposium for the Southwest. She has been awarded over $2 million by external entities for research and innovative projects.

Preface

This special collection is devoted to "Caregiving–Leisure and Aging." Caregiving is an important issue in today's aging society. More older adults need care and more older adults are providing caregiving services. While there is a great deal of literature and research on the topic of caregiving, the combination of aging, caregiving, and leisure is sparse. This special issue blends the work of six manuscripts to: explore aging, caregiving and leisure, and its implications to future practice and research; highlight caregivers and care receivers and their need for leisure and recreation activities; and share innovative recreation programs to help caregivers and care receivers enrich the quality of their lives.

Drs. Cathleen M. Connell and Mary P. Gallant present a review of literature that examines caregivers' health behaviors. Several interventions, home-based exercise and a sleep improvement program were discussed. Also, the notion of self care was highlighted as a potential means to prevent or minimize caregivers' disabilities and impairments. These two authors also highlighted the need for a comprehensive research agenda that helps to understand the impact of health behaviors on caregiving outcomes.

Continuing to review the literature, Dr. Leandra A. Bedini, CTRS and Terri L. Phoenix identified common factors in successful leisure and activities programs for caregivers of older adults. These authors compiled their findings and made recommendations for future practice and research.

Dr. Nancy Brattain Rogers shared in-depth case studies of three women caregivers of older husbands with dementia. Each case illustrated the women's rationale behind sacrificing leisure in order to provide care. Dr. Rogers offered suggestions for practice after addressing the relationship between a strong sense of family obligation and sacrifice of leisure.

A survey of rural and urban caregivers of individuals with probable Alzheimer's disease assessed their educational and support needs. Dr. Linda L. Buettner, CTRS and Sarah Langrish, RN found that rural caregivers and care receivers were older and used fewer services than those in urban settings.

[Haworth indexing entry note]: "Preface." Keller, M. Jean. Published in *Caregiving-Leisure and Aging* (ed: M. Jean Keller) The Haworth Press Inc., 1999, pp. xiii-xiv. Single or multiple copies of this article are available for a fee from The Haworth Document Delivery Service [1-800-342-9678, 9:00 a.m. - 5:00 p.m. (EST). E-mail address: getinfo@haworthpressinc.com].

Caregivers in both urban and rural settings were interested in meaningful activities which could be completed by the individuals for whom they were providing care.

Dr. Marcia Jean Carter, CTRS, CLP, Ida O. Nezey, Karen Wenzel, MA, CTRS, CLP, and Dr. Claire M. Foret, CTRS shared how leisure education offered within the context of support groups can benefit both caregivers and care receivers. Specific leisure education strategies that have been used successfully in caregiver support groups were explained.

An innovative project, Family-Based Structural Multisystem In-home Interventions (FSMII) with a Computer Telephone Integration System (CTIS) is highlighted by Dr. Soledad Argüelles and Adriana von Simson, MSW. This intervention is being used with caregivers of persons with Alzheimer's disease to assist in addressing barriers to accessing and engaging in leisure activities.

"Caregiving–Leisure and Aging" would not have been possible without the contributions from the manuscript's authors. Additionally, an exceptional group of reviewers provided feedback to the authors as to ways they could enhance their articles. The reviewers were: Dr. Gisele Gaudet, Georgia Southern University College of Health and Professional Studies; Dr. Sharon Jacobson, SUNY–Brockport Women's Study Program; Dr. Ted Tedrick, Temple University School of Hospitality and Tourism Management; Dr. Jan Weaver, University of North Texas Center for Public Services and Department of Applied Gerontology; and Dr. Barbara Wilhite, University of North Texas Department of Kinesiology, Health Promotion, and Recreation. My warmest thanks to these outstanding contributors to this special collection. It is our hope that this volume will provide information and ideas regarding the importance of leisure to aging caregivers and care receivers. It is also our hope that this volume will encourage others to expand leisure research and services with aging caregivers and care receivers.

M. Jean Keller, EdD, CTRS
University of North Texas

Caregiver Health Behavior: Review, Analysis, and Recommendations for Research

Cathleen M. Connell
Mary P. Gallant

SUMMARY. Caring for a relative with a chronic illness is an increasingly common experience among families. Although a great deal of evidence links caregiving with adverse health outcomes, the mechanism of this relationship is unclear. One potential mediating factor that has received relatively little research attention is the health behavior patterns of caregivers. The goals of the present paper are to (a) provide a selected review and analysis of the published literature that examines caregiver health behavior, (b) highlight examples of caregiver interventions that include a health behavior component, (c) discuss self care as an appropriate framework for advancing the caregiver literature, and (d) offer recommendations for future research and for the design and evaluation of self care interventions for caregivers. *[Article copies available for a fee from The Haworth Document Delivery Service: 1-800-342-9678. E-mail address: getinfo@haworthpressinc.com <Website: http://www.haworth pressinc.com>]*

KEYWORDS. Self-care, dementia, Alzheimer's disease, self efficacy, nutrition, exercise

---

Cathleen M. Connell, PhD, is Associate Professor, Department of Health Behavior and Health Education, School of Public Health, University of Michigan, Ann Arbor, MI 48109-0489.

Mary P. Gallant, PhD, is Assistant Professor, Department of Health Policy, Management, and Behavior, University at Albany, State University of New York.

The authors would like to acknowledge Benjamin Shaw for his helpful comments on an earlier version of this manuscript.

[Haworth co-indexing entry note]: "Caregiver Health Behavior: Review, Analysis, and Recommendations for Research." Connell, Cathleen M., and Mary P. Gallant. Co-published simultaneously in *Activities, Adaptation & Aging* (The Haworth Press, Inc.) Vol. 24, No. 2, 1999, pp. 1-16; and: *Caregiving–Leisure and Aging* (ed: M. Jean Keller) The Haworth Press, Inc., 1999, pp. 1-16. Single or multiple copies of this article are available for a fee from The Haworth Document Delivery Service [1-800-342-9678, 9:00 a.m. - 5:00 p.m. (EST). E-mail address: getinfo@haworthpressinc.com].

The relationship between caregiving and negative health outcomes has been well documented (for reviews, see Schulz, O'Brien, Bookwala, & Fleissner, 1995; Schulz, Visintainer, & Williamson, 1990; Wright, Clipp, & George, 1993). For example, caregivers are in poorer physical health than age-matched controls (Schulz et al., 1990; Schulz et al., 1995) and often attribute their health problems to the demands of their caregiving responsibilities (Chenoweth & Spencer, 1986; Connell, 1994). Compared to the general population, caregivers consistently report more symptoms and higher rates of depression and anxiety (Schulz et al., 1995).

Despite the awareness of the link between caregiving and adverse physical and mental health outcomes, the mechanism responsible for this relationship is unclear. One potential mediating factor is the health behavior patterns of caregivers. The association between health behaviors and health outcomes is well documented. Physical health status, physical functioning, and mortality are related to physical activity, sleep patterns, proper nutrition, cigarette smoking, alcohol consumption, and maintenance of appropriate body weight (Belloc & Breslow, 1972; Berkman & Breslow, 1983; Buchner, Beresford, Larson, LaCroix & Wagner, 1992; Guralnick, Land, Blazer, Fillenbaum, & Branch, 1993; Habte-Gabr, Wallace, Colsher, Hulbert, White, & Smith, 1991; LaCroix, & Omenn, 1994; Palmore, 1970; Posner, Jette, Smith, & Miller, 1993; Wagner, LaCroix, Buchner, & Larson, 1992). Empirical evidence also suggests that stress influences health behaviors and can lead to increased cigarette smoking, alcohol use, and caloric intake (Conway, Vicker, Ward, & Rahe, 1981; Finney & Moos, 1984; Greeno & Wing, 1994; McCann, Warnick, & Knopp, 1990; Rookus, Burema, & Frijters, 1988).

The relationships among stress, health behaviors and health status may be particularly salient for caregivers. The demands of providing care to a family member may limit opportunities to engage in positive health behaviors, such as exercise, and may promote reliance on negative health behaviors, such as smoking. Because many family caregivers are themselves older adults and are likely to have at least one chronic illness (Guralnik, LaCroix, Everett, & Kovar, 1989), health behaviors may play a vital role in the maintenance and management of their own health.

The goals of the present paper are to: (a) provide a selected review and analysis of the published literature that examines caregiver health behavior, (b) highlight examples of caregiver interventions that include a health behavior component, (c) discuss self care as an appropriate framework for advancing the caregiver literature, and (d) offer recommendations for future research and for the design and evaluation of self care interventions for caregivers.

REVIEW AND ANALYSIS OF THE PUBLISHED LITERATURE THAT EXAMINES CAREGIVER HEALTH BEHAVIOR

Increased attention has been afforded to caregiver health behavior in recent years (see Wright, 1997, for a review). Relevant studies have been conducted from several different vantage points. For example, caregiver health behavior has been compared with that of matched samples of noncaregivers. In several studies, caregivers have been asked whether their health behavior changed since they first began providing care to a family member with a chronic illness. Change over time in caregiver health behavior (i.e., weight gain) has also been examined, using repeated measures and a longitudinal design. In one study, the relationship between caregiver health behaviors and patient cognitive status was examined. Finally, gender differences in the relationships among burden, depression, social support, self-efficacy, and caregiver health behaviors were examined, using a stress and coping model. This literature will be reviewed next.

Burton, Newsom, Schulz, Hirsch, and German (1997) compared health behaviors of 434 caregivers and a sample of 385 noncaregivers, matched for age and gender. All were enrollees in the Cardiovascular Health Study (CHS), a prospective epidemiologic investigation of the incidence of and risk factors for coronary artery disease and stroke among married adults over the age of 65 from four counties in the United States. Results indicated that caregiving was associated with inadequate exercise and rest, not having enough time to rest when sick, forgetting to take medications, and not finding time for doctor appointments. These differences remained even when controlling for age, gender, race, education, self-reported physical health, perceived social support, and sense of control. No significant differences were discovered between caregivers and the comparison group in terms of missed meals, smoking behavior, missed doctor appointments, and missed flu shots. Only one risk behavior, increased use of alcohol, was reported less frequently among caregivers than among noncaregivers. The authors contend that because caregiving interferes with having enough time to rest, exercise, and recuperate, interventions that provide respite and reduce "on duty" hours in the caregiving role may offer a way of promoting preventive health behavior activities. Because the CHS is a longitudinal study, it will be possible to examine the impact of caregiving on preventive health behavior over time.

Schulz, Newsom, Mittelmark, Burton, Hirsch, and Jackson (1997) reported results from a longitudinal study of a population-based sample of 5,888 older adults, including 395 potential caregivers and a group of 424 noncaregivers, matched for age and gender. The authors concluded that caregivers experiencing role strain report substantially elevated levels of depressive symptoms and inadequate time for sleep, self-care, exercise, seeing the doctor, and other health-related activities (Schulz et al., 1997). The authors suggested that promoting positive health behaviors among all caregivers may prevent negative health outcomes (Schulz et al., 1997).

Scharlach, Midanik, Runkle, and Soghikian (1997) examined health behaviors among a sample of 272 caregivers and 917 noncaregivers selected through a stratified random sample of members of a large health maintenance organization in Northern California. After controlling for age, gender, race, education, marital status, and income, results indicated that caregivers were more likely than noncaregivers to eat breakfast daily and get flu shots and pneumonia vaccines. No differences were discovered in terms of getting regular exercise, sleeping moderately (7-8 hours/night), smoking, alcohol use, and body weight. The authors concluded that caregiving responsibilities may not have a deleterious impact on health behaviors, at least for caregivers who have access to extensive health promotion resources.

Baumgarten, Battista, Infante-Rivard, Hanley, Becker, and Gauthier (1992) compared 103 caregivers of family members with dementia to a sample of 115 family members of patients undergoing cataract surgery. Comparisons were made after controlling for gender, age, education, ethnic group, number of chronic diseases, number of stressful life events, coping, social support, and support satisfaction. Although the focus of the study was on the impact of caregiving on depression and physical symptoms, several health behaviors items were included in the interview schedule. Results indicated that caregivers had lower tobacco and alcohol consumption than noncaregivers, but were more likely to be taking at least one psychotropic medication and medication for pain and heartburn (Baumgarten et al., 1992).

Kiecolt-Glaser, Dura, Speicher, Trask, and Glaser (1991) assessed changes in depression, immune function, and health behaviors among 69 spouse caregivers of Alzheimer's patients and 69 control subjects matched for gender, age, and education. Results from their longitudinal study indicated that smoking, alcohol use, and caffeine intake did not differ between the two groups. Caregivers, however, reported getting significantly less sleep in the last three days than control subjects (Kiecolt-Glaser et al., 1991).

Fuller-Jonap and Haley (1995) conducted the only published study of health behaviors among male caregivers of a spouse with Alzheimer's disease and a comparison group of noncaregiving men. The demographic profiles of the two groups were similar; specifically, no differences in age, education, income, and length of marriage were discovered. Compared to the noncaregivers, the caregivers reported more sleep problems and difficulties in getting sufficient rest and exercise. Rates of cigarette smoking or alcohol consumption were similar for the two groups.

Vitaliano, Russo, Scalan, and Greeno (1996) conducted a study to determine weight gain and the prevalence of obesity among a sample of 81 spouse caregivers of people with Alzheimer's disease. Compared to 86 age-matched controls, female caregivers reported significant weight gains over an 18-month period. Male caregivers had greater body mass index and a higher prevalence of obesity than age-matched controls (Vitaliano et al., 1996). In terms of other health behaviors, female caregivers reported significantly less aerobic activity than women in the control group. Caregivers and controls did not differ in the prevalence of current smoking, alcohol use, and caloric and fat intake. Because body mass index and physical inactivity are risk factors for cardiovascular disease, the authors suggested that caregivers are a prime target audience for behavioral interventions (Vitaliano et al., 1996).

In one of the first in-depth studies of the perceived impact of caregiving on health behaviors, Connell (1994) recruited 44 dementia caregivers from one of the 28 federally-funded Alzheimer's Disease Centers. Respondents to a mailed survey indicated whether any of five health behaviors (i.e., nutrition, appetite, exercise, smoking, alcohol use) changed since they first began to provide care to their spouse. Over one-third of the caregivers reported that they ate less nutritiously and 14 percent reported that their appetite had declined since they first provided care for their spouse. Among the 31 caregivers who reported exercising at least once a week, one third reported lower levels of physical activity since they began providing spouse care. Among the 25 caregivers who used alcohol, over one-fourth reported decreasing their alcohol use. Only seven respondents reported being a current smoker, three of whom reported increasing the amount they smoked since first providing care to their spouse.

Respondents were also asked to report how caregiving had affected their health. Commonly mentioned responses included: being tired, exhausted or fatigued; experiencing sleep disturbances; gaining and losing weight; and exercising less frequently. Caregivers also reported the frequency of engaging in specific health behaviors to cope with the stress of caregiving. Over one-half of the sample reported coping by exercising, finding comfort in food, and spending more time sleeping; over one-third of the sample reported taking medications and drinking alcohol. The author concluded that, for some caregivers, providing full-time care to a spouse with a dementing illness decreases the opportunity and/or incentive to engage in preventive health behaviors and increases the prevalence of potentially high risk behaviors (Connell, 1994).

In one of the few studies to assess change over time in caregiver health behavior, Fredman and Daly (1997) examined weight change in 200 informal caregivers to older adults discharged from a rehabilitation hospital. Almost 20% of the sample reported gaining or losing at least 20 pounds since becoming caregivers. Respondents' self-reported weight change since caregiving began was associated with higher levels of caregiver burden, stress, and psychotropic drug use; lower educational level; poorer self-rated physical health; and caring for people with more limitations in activities of daily living. Caregivers to stroke patients (who frequently exhibit symptoms of dementia) reported almost three times more weight change than caregivers to patients with a physical impairment alone (Fredman & Daly, 1997).

Using data collected from older married couples, Moritz, Kasl, and Ostfeld (1992) examined whether selected health behaviors were related to living with a cognitively impaired spouse. Data were from the Yale Health and Aging Project (YHAP), one of four sites involved in the Established Populations for Epidemiologic Studies of the Elderly (EPESE) program. The sample included 318 married couples (636 individuals) from the full YHAP probability sample of 2,812 noninstitutionalized adults over the age of 65 living in New Haven, Connecticut. After controlling for sociodemographic and health factors, results indicated that none of the health behaviors examined (i.e., alcohol use, smoking cigarettes, and drug use) were related to spouses' cognitive functioning.

Gallant and Connell (1997) examined gender differences in predictors of health behaviors (i.e., alcohol consumption, exercise, sleep patterns, smoking, weight maintenance) among a sample of 233 spouse caregivers of dementia patients. Results indicated that the majority of the sample did not drink heavily, although male caregivers were much more likely to drink alcohol frequently and in larger quantities. Almost one-half of the women and one-fourth of the men engaged in physical activity pursuits less than once a week. Two thirds of the women and one-half of the men slept less than seven hours a night. The majority of the sample were nonsmokers (90%) and 70% had a body mass index that was in the ideal range for their age and gender.

Respondents were also asked to assess how their health behaviors changed since caregiving first began (Gallant & Connell, 1997). Very few caregivers reported drinking more since caregiving began; one-fourth of the sample reported drinking less alcohol. Almost one-half of the sample reported being less active now compared to the time before they began providing care to their spouse. A majority of caregivers reported sleeping less since caregiving began and reported gaining or losing weight. Women were significantly more likely than men to report sleeping less and smoking more. In addition, there were significant gender differences in weight change. Almost half of the females reported gaining weight since caregiving began, compared to only 13% of the males. Only half as many females remained the same weight. Multiple regression analyses indicated that caregivers who experienced higher levels of caregiver burden and depression, performed a greater number of activities of daily living tasks in caregiving and spent more hours in a day providing care, and who had lower self-efficacy for both self care and spouse care were at greater risk for negative health behavior change (Gallant & Connell, 1997).

In an expansion of this research, Gallant and Connell (1998) used a stress and coping model to examine the relationship between the demands of providing care to a spouse with dementia and caregiver health behaviors. Structural equation modeling was used to predict health behavior change from personal and environmental characteristics, perceived stress, social support, and depression. Results indicate that depression and caregiver burden were directly related to negative health behavior change. Depression mediated the effects of self-efficacy and objective burden on health behavior change. The authors conclude that the strong links between self-efficacy, depression, and negative health behaviors should be considered in the design of interventions that focus on maintaining and enhancing caregiver health behaviors (Gallant & Connell, 1998).

PUBLISHED LITERATURE

Findings from these studies of the impact of caregiving on health behaviors are not uniform, although the weight of the evidence is strong for some behaviors (e.g., exercise, sleep problems) and weak for others (e.g., smoking, alcohol use). As with the general caregiving literature, differences in sample recruitment, sample size, patient characteristics, and measurement strategies make comparisons across studies very difficult. For example, in some studies, respondents were providing care to a family member with a dementing illness (Baumgarten et al., 1992; Connell, 1994; Fuller-Jonap & Haley, 1995; Gallant & Connell, 1997, 1998; Kiecolt-Glaser et al., 1991; Moritz et al., 1992; Vitaliano, 1996); in others, the impaired person had a non-dementing illness and some limitation in physical functioning, activities of daily living, and/or mobility (Burton et al., 1997; Fredman et al., 1997; Scharlach et al., 1997; Schulz et al., 1997).

In three studies, samples were drawn from large representative samples of older adults (Burton et al., 1997; Moritz et al., 1992; Schulz et al., 1997). In other studies, subjects were recruited from a large health maintenance organization (Scharlach et al., 1997), a large teaching hospital (Baumgarten et al., 1992), from the community (Fuller-Jonap & Haley, 1995; Kiecolt-Glaser et al., 1991; Vitaliano et al., 1996), and from a research center on aging (Fuller-Jonap & Haley, 1995). In studies that did not include a control or comparison group, samples were recruited from a rehabilitation hospital (Fredman et al., 1997) and an Alzheimer's Disease Center (Connell, 1994; Gallant & Connell, 1997, 1998).

Caregiver sample sizes ranged from 44 (Connell, 1994) to 434 (Burton et al., 1997); control samples ranged from 53 (Fuller-Jonap, 1995) to 917 (Scharlach et al., 1997). Structured interviews (Baumgarten et al., 1992; Burton et al., 1997; Fredman & Daly, 1997; Fuller-Jonap & Haley, 1995; Kiecolt-Glaser et al., 1991; Moritz et al., 1992; Schulz et al., 1997) and mailed surveys (Gallant & Connell, 1997, 1998; Scharlach et al., 1997) were commonly used strategies for data collection.

In the majority of studies, health behaviors were assessed with single items rather than scales or indexes. No two studies used identical measures. For example, exercise was assessed by asking respondents: (a) if they "exercise at least three times a week" (Scharlach et al., 1997), (b) if they have "enough time to get as much exercise as they would like" (Burton et al., 1997), and (c) "how often do you do active things in your free time like swimming, taking long walks, doing physical exercises, or working in the garden?" (Gallant & Connell, 1997).

Comparisons in health behaviors between caregivers and matched samples of noncaregivers were drawn in several of the studies. These comparisons were made after controlling for age and education (Baumgarten et al., 1992; Burton et al., 1997; Kiecolt-Glaser et al., 1991; Scharlach et al., 1997), gender (Baumgarten et al., 1992; Burton et al., 1997; Kiecolt-Glaser et al., 1991; Scharlach et al., 1997), race (Burton et al., 1997; Scharlach et al., 1997), ethnicity (Baumgarten et al., 1992), income (Scharlach et al., 1997), marital status (Scharlach et al., 1997), self-rated physical health, perceived social support, and personal control (Burton et al., 1997), and number of chronic diseases, stressful life events, coping, social support, and support satisfaction (Baumgarten et al., 1992).

When taken together, these studies suggest that providing full-time care to a family member with a chronic illness may put caregivers at risk for sleep disturbances, weight gain, and lack of exercise, but may not adversely affect smoking or alcohol consumption. For example, caregivers were found to have significantly more sleep problems (Burton et al., 1997; Fuller-Jonap, 1995; Kiecolt-Glaser et al., 1991; Schulz et al., 1997) and reported exercising less frequently than noncaregivers (Burton et al, 1997; Fuller-Jonap & Haley, 1995; Schulz et al., 1997). Scharlach (1997), however, found no differences between caregivers and noncaregivers in terms of sleep patterns and exercise. In several studies, differences between caregivers and noncaregivers in alcohol use and smoking behavior were not discovered (Burton et al., 1997; Fuller-Jonap, 1995; Kiecolt-Glaser et al., 1991; Scharlach et al., 1997), although lower rates of alcohol and tobacco consumption were reported in one study (Baumgarten et al., 1992). No differences between caregivers and noncaregivers were reported in eating behavior (i.e., appetite, missing meals, caffeine intake, nutrition) (Burton et al., 1997; Kiecolt-Glaser et al., 1991), although one study documented significant weight gain among female caregivers, as compared to controls (Vitaliano et al., 1996). In one of the comparative studies (Scharlach et al., 1997), caregivers belonging to a large health maintenance organization were more likely to report eating breakfast daily and getting a flu shot and pneumonia vaccine than a matched sample of noncaregivers.

In studies without a comparison group, caregivers reported lower levels of exercise (Connell, 1994; Gallant & Connell, 1997) and greater weight gain (Fredman et al., 1997; Gallant & Connell, 1997) since caregiving began. In one study, caregivers reported smoking more, using less alcohol, and poorer nutrition and appetite than before caregiving began (Connell, 1994). Gallant and Connell (1998) reported that higher levels of depression and burden were related to an index of negative health behavior change. Moritz et al. (1992) reported that alcohol use, smoking and drug use were not related to a spouse's cognitive functioning.

CAREGIVER INTERVENTIONS THAT INCLUDE A HEALTH BEHAVIOR COMPONENT

To date, very few interventions that have been reported in the literature have focused exclusively on caregiver health behaviors. Two recent examples are an exception and are described here.

King and Brassington (1997) conducted a population-based survey in the San Francisco Bay area to identify older adults interested in participating in a home-based exercise program. Of 1,526 completed surveys, 103 respondents identified themselves as current family caregivers. Results indicated that physical inactivity was a prevalent risk factor among this group. For example, only 7% of female and 18% of male caregivers reported that they currently exercise. Survey respondents were also asked to rank which of six health promotion activities (i.e., exercise, nutrition, weight control, quitting smoking, stress management, blood pressure control) they were most interested in. Among caregivers, exercise was most frequently ranked as among the top two choices. One third of the women and one-half of the men ranked exercise this highly. For women, weight control was also among the top choices.

Based on these results, King and Brassington (1997) conducted an exploratory study to assess the feasibility and utility of a physical activity program for older caregivers. Of 83 adults who expressed interest in the program, 59 were determined to be ineligible based on study criteria. Of the remaining subjects, 12 adults between the ages of 50 and 75 were randomized to a physical activity training condition and 12 to the wait-list control condition. Although results must be evaluated in light of the small number of participants, King and Brassington (1997) concluded that their study provides initial support for the feasibility of the program as a means to promote increased physical activity among caregivers. Over the four-month program period, participants completed almost 80% of their prescribed exercise sessions. The authors also reported that self-efficacy for exercise was significantly negatively related to perceived caregiver burden, suggesting that efforts to engage in a health enhancing behavior may transfer to other arenas, including perceptions of efficacy in the caregiving role. An important next step will be to replicate this promising program with a large and representative sample of family caregivers.

McCurry, Logsdon, Vitiello and Teri (1998) examined the effectiveness of a brief, multi-component behavioral treatment designed to reduce sleep problems in caregivers of older adults with dementia. In addition to standard training related to sleep problems (i.e., sleep hygiene, stimulus control, sleep compression strategies), the treatment included strategies for managing stress and reducing patient problem behaviors as well as information about community resources. Subjects were recruited from the Seattle area through articles in caregiver and senior newsletters and presentations at senior centers. Of 70 older adults who expressed interest in the study, 57 subjects were deemed eligible and randomly assigned to either a treatment (n = 21) or a wait-list control condition (n = 36). Results indicated that caregiver sleep improved significantly as a result of treatment and that improvements were detected as soon as three weeks following the initial training session.

Both studies addressed common shortcomings in the intervention literature by including a comparison group, establishing strict participant inclusion criteria, and collecting extensive and appropriate measures to evaluate program impact. Although sample sizes for these studies are small, both represent the type of research that will be extremely helpful in guiding the development and implementation of state-of-the-art intervention programs that address the health behaviors of family caregivers.

SELF CARE:
A FRAMEWORK FOR ADVANCING
THE CAREGIVER LITERATURE

Self care has been defined as including "a broad range of behaviors undertaken by individuals, often with the assistance and support of others, that have the intent and effect of maintaining or promoting health and functional independence" (Ory, DeFriese & Duncker, 1998). The concept of self care spans the range of behaviors that individuals use to preserve and enhance their health, including preventive health behaviors, behaviors used to manage chronic illnesses or respond to acute symptoms, and behaviors that facilitate functional independence in the face of impairment. An established literature on self care is available to guide the development and evaluation of interventions designed for caregivers. For example, a recently published edited volume entitled *Self-Care in Later Life: Research, Program, and Policy Issues* describes patterns and processes of self care among older adults, addresses the theoretical underpinnings of self care, and highlights design and evaluation issues (Ory et al., 1998). To date, however, a self care framework has not directly informed the caregiver interventions that appear in the published literature.

Self care interventions with a primary and secondary prevention focus would provide an important complement to the existing array of programs developed for caregivers, including those that provide education and support, behavioral and psychotherapeutic strategies, self-help groups, and respite and adult day care (for reviews, see Knight, Lutzky, & Macofsky-Urban, 1993 and Toseland & Rossiter, 1989). Caregiver self care may prevent or forestall the onset of new health problems, facilitate the self-management of existing illnesses and conditions, and prevent or minimize caregiver impairment. Thus, optimal self care behaviors may extend caregivers' ability to provide full-time in-home care, reduce the likelihood of the patient being institution-alized, and promote positive physical and mental health outcomes for both the caregiver and patient. Because some health behaviors are related in such fundamental ways (e.g., nutrition, weight maintenance, and exercise), focus-ing on multiple behaviors as part of a single intervention may maximize potential positive outcomes. Given the great variability in health status among older adults, interventions that focus on the cross-cutting concept of self care instead of targeting specific behaviors, may be more applicable across a wide variety of populations. The goals of intervention programs designed to promote self care include: (a) to disseminate information about self-care behaviors and behavior change skills, (b) to motivate participants to adopt and maintain appropriate self-care behaviors, (c) to provide timely and meaningful feedback, and (d) to maintain the desired self-care practices and behaviors (Prohaska, 1998; Ory et al., 1998).

Although self care interventions may focus primarily on health behaviors and physical health outcomes (e.g., functional health status, mobility, mortal-ity, morbidity), their impact on caregiver-specific (e.g., burden) and general psychosocial outcomes (e.g., depression, quality of life, life satisfaction) may be equally important. The mechanism by which self care influences psycho-social outcomes may be through an increased sense of personal control over health behaviors, symptoms, or the course of a chronic illness or condition (Affleck, Tennen, Pfeiffer, Fifield, 1987). For some caregivers, maintaining one's overall health status is perceived as an investment in personal well-be-ing and may result in increased sense of mastery, competence, autonomy, and self-reliance (Heurtin-Robert & Becker, 1993; Kart & Engler, 1994; Konrad, 1998; Leventhal & Prohaska, 1986). The limited findings reported here on the role of self efficacy in promoting positive health behavior support the importance of perceptions of personal control. Personal control over some life domains (e.g., caregiver's own physical health) may be especially salient for caregivers of dementia patients because the cognitive and behavioral declines associated with the illness cannot be controlled (Connell, 1994).

RECOMMENDATIONS FOR FUTURE RESEARCH

Future research that examines the health behaviors of caregivers would benefit from attention to several issues. First, based on evidence presented in three of the studies reviewed previously (Gallant & Connell, 1997, 1998; Vitaliano, 1997), gender differences should be expected and consistently examined, especially in the areas of exercise, sleep problems, and weight change. In addition, none of the studies reviewed included sufficient numbers of non-white subjects to present race differences in study results. Because of the mounting evidence of the impact of race, culture and ethnicity on family caregiving (Connell & Gibson, 1997), inclusion of minorities should be a priority for future research. Moreover, there has not been enough attention paid to the influence of race and ethnicity on self care behaviors, or to the differences in self care beliefs and practices among different ethnic groups (Davis & Wykle, 1998).

Future research should also reflect one or more of the theoretical models that have informed both the caregiver and self care literatures (e.g., stress and coping theory, Social Cognitive Theory, self-regulation, Health Belief Model, Theory of Reasoned Action) (Leventhal, Leventhal, & Robitaille, 1998). As discussed by Leventhal et al. (1998), a clear specification of a theoretical framework is important for several reasons. First, interventions based on theory facilitate replication and the interpretation of contradictory findings. Theory also plays a critical role in the identification of contextual factors (e.g., socioeconomic status, gender, self efficacy) that moderate interrelationships and outcomes. In addition, theory is essential for understanding the personal decision-making process resulting in health behavior change.

In the only previously reviewed study to explicitly test a theoretical model based on a stress and coping framework, results suggested that high levels of burden, depression, and caregiving responsibilities are associated with negative health behavior change among dementia caregivers (Gallant & Connell, 1997). Additional research is needed to further explicate the particular paths through which caregiving impacts health behaviors as well as to identify those caregivers who are at greatest risk of deleterious health outcomes among large representative samples of caregivers (Scharlach et al., 1997). For example, the work of Kiecolt-Glaser et al. (1991) suggests that immune functioning is one possible physiological mechanism through which caregiving affects health outcomes.

In addition to a focus on self care as a framework for the design of interventions, much could be learned from research on patterns of leisure activities among older adults. Because the demands of providing full-time care limit available time and energy, caregiving is likely to reduce the opportunity for engaging in a variety of leisure activities (e.g., dancing, shopping, music, hiking, fishing, eating out, walking, gardening) that augment quality of life and contribute to varied and rewarding social relationships and experiences. The links among self care, health behaviors, and leisure activities have yet to be explored in the caregiving literature.

Qualitative approaches to data collection would add to our understanding of the impact of caregiving on health behaviors. Because health behaviors are typically performed on a daily basis, in-depth analysis of health diaries would provide a mechanism to examine short-term change over time and covariation in caregiving demands and health behaviors (Connell & Schulenberg, 1990; Connell, Gallant & Schulenberg, 1991).

Future research would also benefit from greater attention to the measurement of health and self care behavior. The adoption of standardized measures that are appropriate for use with older adults would facilitate comparisons among studies. One approach is to select measures that have been used in large studies of the general population that have linked health behaviors with positive health outcomes, including those from the Alameda County Study (Belloc & Breslow, 1972; Berkman & Breslow, 1983). Another strategy is to use measures that have been developed and tested as part of large scale intervention programs. Although most of the studies reviewed here relied on single-item measures of health behaviors, complex behaviors such as exercise cannot be captured with sufficient accuracy with a single item. Greater attention should be afforded to the development of multi-item measures of preventive health behaviors.

The aging of the population ensures that an increasing number of adults will serve as a caregiver to a chronically ill family member. Given the well documented relationship between health behaviors and overall health status and the successful efforts in modifying high risk behaviors as part of intervention programs, a focus on a broad range of self care behaviors in the caregiver literature is clearly warranted. Future research that incorporates standardized measures, utilizes large and representative samples, examines gender differences, includes sufficient numbers of non-white participants to assess differences by race, culture, and/or ethnicity, includes leisure activities, considers qualitative approaches, and is informed by the existing literature on self care theory and interventions will make a major contribution to our understanding of the impact of health behaviors on caregiving outcomes.

REFERENCES

Affleck, G., Tennen, H., Pfeiffer, C., & Fifield, J. (1987). Appraisals of control and predictability in adapting to a chronic disease. *Journal of Personality and Social Psychology, 53*, 273-279.

Baumgarten, M., Battista, R. N., Infante-Rivard, C., Hanley, J. A., Becker, R., & Gauthier, S. (1992). The psychological and physical health of family members caring for an elderly person with dementia. *Journal of Clinical Epidemiology, 45*, 61-70.

Belloc, N. B. & Breslow, L. (1972). Relationship of physical health status and health practices. *Preventive Medicine, 1*, 409-421.

Berkman, L. F. & Breslow, L. (1983). *Health and ways of living: The Alameda County Study.* New York: Oxford University Press.

Buchner, D. M., Beresford, S. A., Larson, E. B., LaCroix, A. Z., & Wagner, E. H. (1992). Effects of physical activity on health status in older adults. II. Intervention studies. *Annual Review of Public Health, 13*, 469-488.

Burton, L. C., Newsom, J. T., Schulz, R., Hirsch, C. H., & German, P. S. (1997). Preventive health behaviors among spousal caregivers. *Preventive Medicine, 26*, 162-169.

Chenoweth, B. & Spencer, B. (1986). Dementia: The experience of family caregivers. *The Gerontologist, 26*, 267-272.

Connell, C. M. (1994). Impact of spouse caregiving on health behaviors and physical and mental health status. *American Journal of Alzheimer's Disease, 9*, 26-36.

Connell, C. M. & Gibson, G. D. (1997). Racial, ethnic, and cultural differences in dementia caregiving: Review and analysis. *The Gerontologist, 37*, 355-364.

Connell, C. M., & Schulenberg, J. (1990). Daily variation in the physical and mental health impact of caregiving. *The Gerontologist, 30*, 236A.

Connell, C. M., Gallant, M. P., & Schulenberg, J. (1991). Daily variation in caregiving hassles: A factor analytic approach. *The Gerontologist, 31*, 193A.

Conway, T. L., Vickers, R. R., Jr., Ward, H. W., & Rahe, R. H. (1981). Occupational stress and variation in cigarette, coffee, and alcohol consumption. *Journal of Health and Social Behavior, 22*, 155-165.

Davis, L. & Wykle, M. L. (1998). Self-care in minority and ethnic populations: The experience of older black americans. In M. G. Ory & G. H. DeFriese (Eds.), *Self-care in later life: Research, program, and policy issues.* New York: Springer Publishing Company, Inc., pgs. 170-179.

Finney, J. W. & Moos, R. H. (1984). Life stressors and problem drinking among older adults. In M. Galanter (Ed.), *Recent developments in alcoholism.* New York: Plenum, pgs. 267-288.

Fredman, L. & Daly, M. P. (1997). Weight change: An indicator of caregiver stress. *Journal of Aging and Health, 9*, 43-69.

Fuller-Jonap, F. & Haley, W. E. (1995). Mental and physical health of male caregivers of a spouse with Alzheimer's disease. *Journal of Aging and Health, 7*, 99-118.

Gallant, M. P. & Connell, C. M. (1997). Predictors of decreased self-care among spouse caregivers of older adults with dementing illness. *Journal of Aging and Health, 9*, 373-395.

Gallant, M. P. & Connell, C. M. (1998). The stress process among dementia spouse caregivers: Are caregivers at risk for negative health behavior change? *Research on Aging, 20,* 267-297.

Greeno, C. B. & Wing, R. R. (1994). Stress-induced eating. *Psychological Bulletin, 115,* 444-464.

Guralnick, J. M., LaCroix, A. Z., Everett, D., & Kovar, M. (1989). *Advance data, aging in the eighties: The prevalence of comorbidity and its association with disability.* Hyattsville, MD: U.S. Department of Health and Human Services.

Guralnick, J. M., Land, K. C., Blazer, D., Fillenbaum, G. G,. & Branch, L. G. (1993). Education status and active life expectancy among older blacks and whites. *The New England Journal of Medicine, 329,* 2, 110-116.

Habte-Gabr, E., Wallace, R. B., Colsher, P. L., Hulbert, J. R., White, L. R., & Smith, I. M. (1991). Sleep patterns in rural elders: Demographic, health and psychobehavioral correlates. *Journal of Clinical Epidemiology, 44,* 5-13.

Heurtin-Roberts, S. & Becker, G. (1993). Anthropological perspective on chronic illness: Introduction. *Social Science and Medicine, 37,* 281-283.

Kart, C. & Engler, C. (1994). Predisposition to self-health care: Who does what for themselves and why. *Journal of Gerontology: Social Sciences, 49,* 6, S301-S308.

Kielcolt-Glaser, J. K., Dura, J. R., Speicher, C. E., Trask, O. J., & Glaser, R. (1991). Spousal caregivers of dementia victims: Longitudinal changes in immunity and health. *Psychosomatic Medicine, 53,* 345-362.

King, A. C. & Brassington, G. (1997). Enhancing physical and psychological functioning in older family caregivers: The role of regular physical activity. *Annals of Behavioral Medicine, 19,* 91-100.

Knight, B. G., Lutzky, S. M., & Mcofsky-Urban, F. (1993). A meta-analytic review of interventions for caregiver distress: Recommendations for future research. *The Gerontologist, 33,* 240-248.

Konrad, T. R. (1998). The patterns of self-care among older adults in western industrialized societies. In M. G. Ory & G. H. DeFriese (Eds.), *Self-care in later life: Research, program, and policy issues* (pp. 1-23). New York: Springer Publishing Company, Inc.

LaCroix, A. Z. & Omenn, G. S. (1994). Older adults and smoking. *Clinical Geriatric Medicine, 8,* 69-87.

Leventhal, E. & Prohaska, T. (1986). Age, symptom interpretation and health behavior. *Journal of the American Geriatrics Society, 34,* 185-191.

Leventhal, E. A., Leventhal, H., & Robitaille, C. (1998). Enhancing self-care research: Exploring the theoretical underpinnings of self-care. In M. G. Ory & G. H. DeFriese, G. H. (Eds.), *Self-care in later life: Research, program, and policy issues.* New York, NY: Springer Publishing Company, Inc., pgs. 118-141.

McCann, B. S., Warnick, R., & Knopp, R. H. (1990). Changes in plasma lipids and dietary intake accompanying shifts in perceived workload and stress. *Psychosomatic Medicine, 52,* 97-108.

McCurry, S. M., Logsdon, R. G., Vitiello, M. V., & Teri, L. (1998). Successful behavioral treatment for reported sleep problems in elderly caregivers of dementia patients: A controlled study. *Journal of Gerontology: Psychological Sciences, 53B,* P122-P129.

Moritz, D. J., Kasl, S. V., & Ostfeld, A. M. (1992). The health impact of living with a cognitively impaired elderly spouse: Blood pressure, self-rated health, and health behaviors. *Journal of Aging and Health, 4*, 244-267.

Ory, M. G., DeFriese, G. H., & Duncker, A. P. (1998). Introduction: The nature, extent, and modifiability of self-care behaviors in later life. In M. G. Ory & G. H. DeFriese (Eds.), *Self-care in later life: Research, program, and policy issues* (pp. xv-xxvi). New York: Springer Publishing Company, Inc.

Palmore, E. B. (1970). Health practices and illness among the aged. *The Gerontologist, 10*, 313-316.

Posner, B. M., Jette, A. M., Smith, K. W., & Miller, D. R. (1993). Nutrition and health risks in the elderly: The nutrition screening initiative. *American Journal of Public Health, 83*, 972-978.

Prohaska, T. (1998). The research basis for the design and implementation of self-care programs. In M. G. Ory & G. H. DeFriese, G. H. (Eds.), *Self-care in later life: Research, program, and policy issues* (pp. 62-84). New York, NY: Springer Publishin g Company, Inc.

Rookus, M. A., Burema, J., & Frijters, J. E. (1988). Changes in body mass index in young adults in relation to number of life events experienced. *International Journal of Obesity, 12*, 29-39.

Scharlach, A. E., Midanik, L. T., Runkle, M. C., & Soghikian, K. (1997). Health practices of adults with elder care responsibilities. *Preventive Medicine, 26*, 155-161.

Schulz, R., Newsom, J., Mittelmark, M., Burton, L., Hirsch, C., & Jackson, S. (1997). Health effects of caregiving: The caregiver health effects study: An ancillary study of the Cardiovascular Health Study. *Annals of Behavioral Medicine, 19*, 110-116.

Schulz, R., O'Brien, A. T., Bookwala, J., & Fleissner, K. (1995). Psychiatric and physical morbidity effects of dementia caregiving: Prevalence, correlates, and causes. *The Gerontologist, 35*, 771-791.

Schulz, R., Visintainer, P., & Williamson, G. M. (1990). Psychiatric and physical morbidity effects of caregiving. *Journal of Gerontology, 45*, 181-191.

Toseland, R. W. & Rossiter, C. M. (1989). Group interventions to support family caregivers: A review and analysis. *The Gerontologist, 29*, 438-448.

Vitaliano, P. P., Russo, J., Scanlan, J. M., & Greeno, C. G. (1996). Weight changes in caregivers of Alzheimer's care recipients: Psychobehavioral predictors. *Psychology and Aging, 11*, 155-163.

Wagner, E. D., LaCroix, A. Z., Bucher, D. M., & Larson, E. B. (1992). Effects of physical activity on health status in older adults. I. Observational studies. *Annual Review of Public Health, 13*:451-468.

Wright, L. K. (1997). Health behavior of caregivers. In E. S. Gochman (Ed.), *Handbook of health behavior research III: Demography, development, and diversity.* New York: Plenum Press, pgs. 267-284.

Wright, L. K., Clipp, E. C., & George, L. K. (1993). Health consequences of caregiver stress: *Medicine, Exercise, Nutrition, and Health, 2*, 181-195.

Recreation Programs
for Caregivers of Older Adults:
A Review and Analysis
of Literature from 1990 to 1998

Leandra A. Bedini
Terri L. Phoenix

SUMMARY. Due to social, economic, and medical factors, more adults are choosing to care for ill or disabled relatives at home. Although leisure and recreation have particular benefits for informal family caregivers of older adults, caregivers often have limited social and leisure lives. The purpose of this paper is to use an integrative review technique (Jackson, 1980) to identify common factors in recreation and leisure and related programs for caregivers of older adults. A total of 22 journal articles were reviewed yielding five categories of programs. All programs were reviewed separately and recommendations for practice and future research are presented. *[Article copies available for a fee from The Haworth Document Delivery Service: 1-800-342-9678. E-mail address: getinfo@ haworthpressinc.com <Website: http://www.haworthpressinc.com>]*

KEYWORDS. Caregivers, leisure, programs, respite, social, intervention

Many factors are enhancing the longevity of older adults in the United States; however, living longer often brings with it illnesses or diseases related

Leandra A. Bedini is Associate Professor and Terri L. Phoenix is a master's degree candidate, Department of Recreation, Parks, and Tourism, University of North Carolina at Greensboro, 420 C HHP Building, P.O. Box 26169, Greensboro, NC 27402-6169.

[Haworth co-indexing entry note]: "Recreation Programs for Caregivers of Older Adults: A Review and Analysis of Literature from 1990 to 1998." Bedini, Leandra A., and Terri L. Phoenix. Co-published simultaneously in *Activities, Adaptation & Aging* (The Haworth Press, Inc.) Vol. 24, No. 2, 1999, pp. 17-34; and: *Caregiving-Leisure and Aging* (ed: M. Jean Keller) The Haworth Press, Inc., 1999, pp. 17-34. Single or multiple copies of this article are available for a fee from The Haworth Document Delivery Service [1-800-342-9678, 9:00 a.m. - 5:00 p. m. (EST). E-mail address: getinfo@haworthpressinc.com].

to aging. As a result, more adults are finding themselves caring for ill or disabled family members in their homes without pay. Additionally, these informal family caregivers (Cantor, 1983) are finding themselves with multiple roles such as being employed and having to care for children. To attempt to juggle these many responsibilities as well as the burden of caregiving, many informal family caregivers abandon or greatly reduce their recreation and leisure pursuits. This is a great concern to professionals who do or can provide leisure and recreation opportunities for this population.

Leisure has been found to provide unique benefits to people of all ages and situations. For example, leisure can serve as a buffer to stress (Coleman & Iso-Ahola, 1993). Therefore, leisure and recreation have particular benefits for caregivers of older adults. Unfortunately, caregivers have limited social lives; engage in few recreation activities, go out to dinner rarely, and infrequently visit with friends (Thompson, Futterman, Gallagher-Thompson, Rose, & Lovett, 1993; Wilson, 1990).

Much of the caregiver literature of the 1980s cited a desire for leisure identified by caregivers (e.g., Bedini & Bilbro, 1991) but rarely identified research that explored these needs and perceptions. Caregivers seemed to want recreation and leisure in their lives, but because of a variety of barriers and stigmas due to caregiving, they had reduced or forsaken it altogether (Bedini & Guinan, 1996). Although some recreation and leisure programs have been developed for caregivers, "The literature is silent on the relative effectiveness of social, recreational, educational, service, and advocacy groups [for caregivers]" (McCallion & Toseland, 1995, p. 22). Therefore, the purpose of this paper is to use an integrative review methodology to identify common factors in successful recreation and leisure and related programs for caregivers of older adults and compile recommendations for practice and future research about these and similar programs. For the purposes of this study leisure was defined as social activities, hobbies, relaxation, recreation, and free time activities.

METHODS

An integrative review technique (Jackson, 1980) was implemented to conduct this analysis. According to Jackson (1980), an integrative review ". . . should explore the reasons for the differences in the results and determine what the body of research, taken as a whole, reveals and does not reveal about the topic" (p. 439). Six refereed journals dealing with recreation/leisure and/or aging published between the years of 1990 and 1998 were reviewed to identify articles that addressed the topics of caregiving and programs in recreation, leisure, or social support that facilitated the pursuit of leisure. Articles were solicited from *Activities, Adaptation & Aging, Annual in Ther-*

apeutic Recreation, Journal of Gerontology, Journal of Gerontological Social Work, The Gerontologist, and the Therapeutic Recreation Journal. Additionally, six databases (CINAHL, ERIC, Medline, PsycLIT, Social Sciences
Abstracts, and Sport Discus) were searched for the identified topics. Key
words for the search included leisure, recreation, interventions, programs,
activities, socializing, hobbies, free time, leisure education, unobligated time,
caregivers, elderly, aging, and strategies. A total of 22 journal articles which
met the criteria (i.e., addressed programs in recreation, leisure, or social
support that facilitated the pursuit of leisure for caregivers of older adults)
were identified and reviewed for this study. The articles included both proposed as well as empirically tested programs and models, and addressed
leisure and recreation as either the primary focus or a secondary finding of
the research. The review analysis questions addressed purpose of study,
theoretical/conceptual framework, methods used, conclusions, effectiveness
of programs analyzed, and implications and recommendations for both researchers and practitioners. Data analysis consisted of constant comparison
technique (Henderson, 1991) whereby two researchers read through all the
articles, sorted them into topical categories, and analyzed them based on the
integrative review questions identified above (i.e., purpose, framework,
methods, results, implications).

SUMMARY OF FINDINGS

A total of 22 journal articles were reviewed to determine the status and
successfulness of programs that provided training, opportunity, or time for
the leisure and recreation of caregivers of older adults. Five groups or categories were identified by this procedure. Category topics included interventions
(n = 2), respite (n = 5), support groups (n = 4), education/training (n = 4), and
a combination of support group and education-training group (n = 7).

Purpose

Fourteen of the 22 articles scientifically evaluated the effectiveness of a
leisure, recreation, or social support program for caregivers of older adults.
Only one article actually tested the effect of a leisure/recreation program
specifically. Overall topics within the articles included subjective burden (n = 7),
support networks (n = 5), social support (n = 4), knowledge and use of
community services (n = 4), time use (n = 2), activity restriction (n = 2), life
satisfaction (n = 1), life upset (n = 1), and self-care (n = 1). Seven articles
proposed the benefits or effectiveness of selected programs based on literature and conceptual logic, however, were not empirically tested. These topics

included balance of caring responsibilities for self and care-recipient (n = 5); leisure information, skills, and resources (n = 4); identifying and using community resources (n = 3); social support (n = 2); social network (n = 2); relief of caregiver burden (n = 1); decreasing leisure constraints (n = 1); and leisure involvement (n = 1). The remaining article described an assessment tool that dealt with perceived social support and had direct implications for the leisure of caregivers of older adults.

Theoretical/Conceptual Base

Theoretical or conceptual frameworks are sets of logically related statements that explain phenomena and offer guidance for the process of conducting research (e.g., Fawcett & Downs, 1986; Henderson, 1991). Six of the articles presented a sum total of seven different conceptual or theoretical frameworks. Fourteen articles presented rationales for the programs described through literature reviews that ranged from a few paragraphs to several pages. They did not present any theoretical or conceptual framework, however. One article discussed a review of programs but indicated no conceptual framework on which they were built. The six articles that used conceptual frameworks presented theories such as stress theories, crisis theory, and the stress-buffer hypothesis; however, they did not cite references. Other articles based their programs on models such as the Model of Linkages (Noelker & Bass, 1989), the Leisure Education Model (Peterson & Gunn, 1984), or the Open Systems' Model (Schopler & Galinsky, 1993).

Methods Used

Seven different research methods or combinations of methods were used in the articles that tested the effectiveness of the programs proposed. They included interviews and questionnaires (n = 7); questionnaires alone (n = 2); focus groups (n = 2); in-depth interviews (n = 1); experimental design with control group (n = 1); observations and interviews (n = 1); and a combination of observations, questionnaires, and interviews (n = 1). Scales and instruments used in these studies included the "Yesterday Interview" (Moss & Lawton, 1982) Subjective Burden Scale (Zarit, Reever, & Bach-Peterson, 1980), Support Network Checklist (Enright & Friss, 1987), Life Satisfaction Index (Wood, Wylie, & Sheafor, 1969), Jaloweic Coping Scale (Jaloweic, Murphy, & Powers, 1984), Montgomery-Borgatta Burden Scale (Montgomery & Borgatta, 1986), Life Restriction Scale (Poulshock & Deimling, 1984), and Stokes Social Network Scale (Stokes, 1983). Additionally, several self-developed scales on coping, perceived social support, and stress were used.

Results and Conclusions

The five categories of programs were: (a) interventions, (b) respite, (c) support groups, (d) education/training, and (e) education-training/ support group combination. Each will be presented separately for what we learned from these articles as grouped.

Intervention. The first category of articles presented two different recreation interventions; one in music and one in horticulture therapy. Both of these articles noted the potential of the recreation interventions to relieve stress and burden in caregivers of older adults and to improve the relationship between the caregiver and the care-recipient through joint participation in the intervention described. Smith and McCallion (1997) described a horticulture therapy program for caregivers of frail elderly. Proposed benefits of this program were that the caregivers were present in the home, it was flexible to caregiving demands, the cost was low, and it built upon existing interests and skills of the caregivers. Although no testing was conducted for this program, the authors presented anecdotal evidence from the literature to support suggested positive outcomes. For example, they estimated the success of a horticulture therapy program since other studies found that plants decreased the use of pain medications, assisted in post-surgical recovery, and increased positive behaviors and affect (e.g., Sneha & Trista, 1991; Williams, 1989). The authors suggested that in providing this type of intervention, it is important to assess what type of gardening activities the caregivers currently enjoyed or had enjoyed before becoming caregivers. Additionally, they recommended that the caregiver determine how functional the home is for beginning and maintaining horticulture activities (i.e., light, space, storage, irrigation). Finally, they suggested that caregivers consider to what extent the care-recipient can participate if the one of the goals of intervention is joint participation.

Dupuis and Pedlar (1995) discussed the role that a structured family leisure program played in enhancing family visits and alleviating caregiver burden for family members of institutionalized older adults with Alzheimer's disease. The specific structured leisure program presented in this study was a family music program which took place during family visits with their care-recipients. The authors proposed that the benefits of this type of shared music program would include facilitation of communication and perhaps bring family members closer together. Although the content of the sessions varied based on the interests of the family group, the structure of the sessions was consistent. For example, the music session began with greetings to each participant and then a greeting song. A topic for the session was introduced and briefly discussed. Then songs relevant to a chosen topic were used to help evoke memories and enhance discussion. The final 20 minutes of each session were reserved for playing and singing residents' and family members' favorite songs. The described music program was tested with evaluation methods to determine its effectiveness on four residents and their family groups. Data were collected through examining the results of structured observations of the residents' facial and bodily expressions, behaviors, and interactions with family members, staff, and other residents. Additionally, post intervention, in-depth interviews were conducted with family members. The authors identified four resulting outcomes: (a) enhanced quality of visits, (b) leisure programs as serving as social support, (c) leisure programs as serving as coping mechanisms, and (d) enriched relationships.

In summary, the two articles about interventions for caregivers of older adults can help service providers understand several things. First, for interventions to be effective, they need to be of interest to the participant. Second, interventions that facilitate positive caregiver and care-recipient interactions can strengthen and improve these relationships. Third, these interventions can serve as a context for development of social networks. Finally, the above mentioned interventions have the potential to decrease stress of caregiving by providing positive and enjoyable experiences.

Respite. Five articles addressed the second category, respite care, as an avenue to providing free time and time for leisure specifically for caregivers of older adults. The foci of these articles included time use during respite, activity participation during respite, sample respite programs, use of programmed videos to provide respite, and evaluation of a model respite program for caregiver well-being.

One of the articles described respite programs that had been developed but not empirically tested. Feinberg and Kelly (1995) described five types of respite programs currently used in California's Caregiver Resource Centers. These programs included in-home care, adult day care, overnight respite, weekend retreats, and other respite options such as emergency respite and respite transportation subsidies. Although no formal evaluation was conducted, the authors reported that annual client satisfaction surveys were consistently positive and attributed this satisfaction to flexibility, choice, and consumer control.

Four articles described empirical studies which examined or measured the effectiveness of different types of respite programs on caregivers' time use, activity participation, and reduction of burden. Lund, Hill, Caserta and Wright (1995) presented a "Video-Respite" program in which video tapes created specifically for individuals with dementia were used to capture their attention, thus providing caregivers opportunities for free time. Pilot study video tapes filmed actual family members who "interacted" with their care-recipient via the video. Results from the pilot study suggested that the video tapes did engage the care-recipients' attention and the caregivers had increased free time as a result of the video's effectiveness. A larger implementation of this same study used generic videos rather than custom made versions with family members. Preliminary results showed that over three-quarters of the care-recipients attended well and that 67% of the caregivers used the videos as a way to create respite time for themselves. An additional benefit from these videos was that caregivers had the opportunity to attend support groups knowing their respective care-recipients were engaged by the video in a nearby room.

Moss, Lawton, Kleban, and Duhamel (1993) examined time use and activity participation by caregivers before and after the institutionalization of their care-recipients. The authors asked subjects to complete a time budget called the "Yesterday Interview" which asked the subjects to recount all activities they participated in the day before. The activities were grouped into three main categories: (a) direct assistance to the care-recipient, (b) obligated time (necessary for caregiver survival such as self-care, house care), and (c) discretionary activities, such as self chosen recreation or social interactions. Results showed that when the care-recipient was institutionalized, there was a statistically significant decrease in the amount of time spent helping the care-recipients as well as increased time toward discretionary activities. Specifically, recreation showed a statistically significant increase of 23 minutes per day after the care-recipient was moved to a nursing home. Also, the results showed an increase in social time with members of the household and an increase in time spent outside of the home following the care-recipient's move to a nursing home.

Berry, Zarit, and Rabatin (1991) conducted a comparative analysis of female caregivers who used home care and day care for respite. A modified version of the "Yesterday Interview" was used in this study as well. Three categories identified included (a) caregiving with the patient, (b) caregiving without the patient, and (c) non-caregiving activities. Differences between adult day care and home care caregivers were found in life satisfaction, quality of caregiver/care-recipient relationships, and time spent away from the care-recipient. Home respite users demonstrated higher ratings on life satisfaction and quality of relationships, however, adult day care users reported more time away from the care-recipients. Ironically, caregivers who used day care respite spent more time on caregiving activities but respite provided large blocks of free time to pursue other activities. A notable result, however, is that the free time provided by respite was mostly spent working or catching up on chores rather than engaging in family or social activities.

Deimling (1992) documented the effects of respite on caregivers of patients with Alzheimer's disease regarding care related strain, depression, health, and activity restriction. Findings showed a significant decrease in depression and a decrease in activity restriction as a result of respite. Moderate amounts of respite, however, did not provide adequate time for caregivers to pursue social and recreational activities. Rather, caregivers did "catch-up" work and chores. The author suggested that larger blocks of time would be necessary for caregivers to pursue their leisure.

Overall, the research about respite programs and their effect on recreation and social activities and pursuits of caregivers is fairly consistent. First, respite does increase time for caregivers to pursue "other" activities. This time, in turn, may affect satisfaction levels of caregivers. When providing respite to caregivers of older adults, it is important to provide large amounts of time through in order to encourage recreation pursuits. The most successful use of respite for providing recreation opportunities, according to these studies, was the transfer of the care-recipient to a nursing home.

Support groups. Four articles addressed support groups as a factor that affected caregivers' social and recreational opportunities and pursuits. Three of these were studies that measured the effectiveness of model programs on psychosocial variables and situational factors that dealt with life satisfaction, social networks, or social support. The fourth article described the development of an instrument to measure perceived social support of caregivers of adults with Alzheimer's disease.

Burks, Lund, and Hill (1991) questioned 490 caregivers about benefits of caregiver support groups. Results showed that there existed a positive correlation between the number of support group meetings attended and higher sense of perceived help as well as caregivers' use of community services. Interestingly, the more meetings attended also correlated with decreased life satisfaction. The researchers were not able to determine a predisposition regarding life satisfaction, however. This study suggested that those caregivers who attended too many or too few support group meetings were also at risk. In light of these issues, the authors suggested that caregiver support group organizers consider topics broader than just caregiving responsibilities to address potential issues of life satisfaction.

Mittleman et al. (1995) examined the effects of a comprehensive support program on the depression of spousal caregivers. Specifically, the level of caregiver satisfaction with social networks was examined as a measure of program effectiveness. Results showed that the effect of increase in caregivers' satisfaction with social networks through social groups led to decreases in levels of depression.

Thompson, Futterman, Gallagher-Thompson, Rose, and Lovett (1993) examined the relationship among six types of social support and five types of caregiver burden. The six types of social support examined were: (a) intimate interaction, (b) material aid, (c) advice, (d) supportive feedback, (e) physical assistance, and (f) social participation. To measure social participation, the authors developed the Social Life Restriction Scale (modified from Poulshock & Deimling, 1984) which included recreation and leisure participation.

In discussing the findings, the authors stated that not all types of social support were equally helpful in reducing caregiver burden. They summarized the results of the study by stating, "Engaging in social interaction for fun and recreation appears to be the most important in diminishing the burden of caregiving" (p. S245).

Goodman (1991) developed an instrument to measure perceived social support of caregivers of adults with Alzheimer's disease based on the stress-buffer hypothesis. The development of the scale was based on context from Leiberman's (1979) benefits of support groups (i.e., emotional support, catharsis, information and guidance, links to practical assistance, and simulation of problems). Factor analysis and subsequent statistical analyses found evidence of validity and reliability to measure perceived social support with this scale.

In summary, support groups seem to have potential for many benefits (e.g., the perception of getting help as well as emotional support, and the identification and use of resources and information). It is important, however, to examine and match the types of support provided to the needs and situations of the caregivers.

Education/Training. Three of four articles in this category specifically addressed the role of leisure education as a valuable tool to facilitate caregivers' coping mechanisms. Keller and Hughes (1991) and Hughes and Keller (1992) proposed that provision of leisure education programs within a caregivers' support group context could facilitate caregiver leisure participation. The authors noted that leisure participation can increase coping behaviors among caregivers of people with Alzheimer's disease, however, barriers often prevent leisure participation by caregivers. They proposed a leisure education program based on the Peterson and Gunn Leisure Education Model (1984) which offers four components: leisure awareness, leisure activity skills, knowledge and awareness of leisure resources, and social skills. An education program, such as the one proposed, can address and remove barriers to leisure, thus increasing opportunities for leisure participation. The authors also suggested that a leisure education program can help the caregivers balance time and responsibility for care of the care-recipients and themselves. Additionally, this proposed program can help caregivers adjust to changes and constraints that caregiving places on their leisure involvement. Finally, a leisure education program can assist caregivers in identifying personal, family, and community resources that could enable them to engage in meaningful leisure experiences while providing care.

Hagan, Green, and Starling (1997/98) also described a leisure education program that was designed to reduce the stress associated with caregiving. They offered three specific goals of the program: (a) provide an opportunity to develop personal time management skills, (b) provide an opportunity to gain knowledge related to leisure activities, and (c) provide an opportunity to gain knowledge related to leisure and support resources. The program content and design consisted of a progression of five levels or components lasting 90 minutes each. The authors stated that the program could be implemented through support groups and care groups for families at hospitals, nursing homes, skilled nursing facilities, and Alzheimer's disease specialty units. The primary components of the model included time management, identification of leisure interests, identification of resources, and application of leisure skills. The authors suggested that the benefits, in addition to the identified goals, included increased leisure participation as well as increased social networks.

The last article of this group empirically tested a program called the Caregiver Support Project. Barusch and Spaid (1991) designed a study that provided 6-week sessions aimed at increasing coping skills and decreasing the sense of burden that comes from caregiving. Two groups were tested: family member participation condition (caregiver brought a family member), and the individual condition (caregiver came alone). Data were collected through interviews of each caregiver, Zarit et al.'s (1980) measure of subjective burden, and a self-developed 34 item coping inventory. Results indicated a small (4%) amount of improvement in all treatment groups but no difference between the family participation condition and the independent condition. Also, caregiver coping effectiveness demonstrated a statistically significant improvement of 18%. Since there was no control group in this study, however, the effects of maturation cannot be completely distinguished from treatment effects. Although it remains unclear whether there was increased benefit by involving family members (as opposed to only caregivers), caregivers did show an increase in coping skills, and a decrease in subjective burden as a result of participation in the Caregiver Support Project.

In summary, only one model was tested from the education/training group of articles, but that study provided support for the education/training approach to addressing caregiver leisure needs. Interesting to note, the empirical study found that a group approach was superior to the in-home/one on one approach. It is possible, due to this result, that there was an added effect of social support accompanying training for this group. The one on one leisure education model suggested group formats as well. The rationale is strong for giving people information directed at alleviating barriers as well as providing/encouraging support for leisure/recreation pursuits. The potential benefits of education/training as proposed by these articles include increased use of community resources, increased time management, increased social networks, decreased subjective burden, and increased coping skills.

Combination of education/training and support groups. A total of seven articles made up this group. Three of the articles described programs that

combined an education or training component with a support group component. Smyth and Harris (1993) presented a telecomputing (computing
through telephone lines) based project designed to provide not only information (i.e., about Alzheimer's disease), but also support through functions such
as chat rooms. The authors argued that using computers offered many benefits to caregivers regarding education and support. In addition to the obvious
benefits of information, telecomputing offered an opportunity to communicate with others and to gain resources independently from within their own
homes. Additionally, telecomputing allowed caregiver anonymity. The project described had several components. Participants could learn about the
Alzheimer's Disease Support Center in Cleveland that sponsored this project.
Also, users could find common questions and answers about topics such as
dementia, treatment, and behavior. The information rack provided users with
bibliographies, video lists, and brochures that can be ordered. A bulletin
board about Alzheimer's disease was also available. The Caregiver Forum
included helpful hints for caregivers as well as an electronic support group.

Two articles described educational support groups for caregivers of older
adults; one in the community and one in a hospital. McCallion and Toseland
(1995) described four categories of group interventions: (a) mutual support
groups; (b) psycho-educational groups; (c) social, recreational, and education
groups; and (d) service and advocacy groups. Mutual support groups provided opportunities for caregivers to come together to discuss common concerns and share information. Psycho-educational groups, on the other hand,
utilized and identified a leader and focused on problem-solving to address
specific issues. Additionally, the psycho-education groups had specific goals
and specific agendas for the meetings. The social, recreational, and educational group was identified as perhaps the most important group. The authors
stated, "Of all the kinds of social support available to caregivers of the frail
elderly, some evidence suggests that the most important is the opportunity to
socialize and be engaged with friends, family and acquaintances" (p. 17).
The last category, service and advocacy groups, allowed the caregivers an
opportunity to engage in meaningful social roles. In the context of advocating
for services or interests of caregivers, social relationships among caregivers
are formed and provide a forum to make use of and pass on their experiences,
strength, and hope in caregiving. The authors stressed how these group interventions provided an arena for addressing specific concerns or issues as well
as increasing the social network of caregivers.

Hamlet and Read (1990) reviewed the goals, development, and evaluation
of a caregiver education and support group provided through the local hospital in which the care-recipient was a patient. Ninety minute sessions focused
on group determined topics such as interpersonal relationships, coping with
personal feelings, and utilization of community resources. The education and

support group presented educational information on these topics as well as provided for open discussion among participants. This program was able to address needs of two different caregiver types: those who sought specific information about caregiving responsibilities, and those who wanted long-term emotional support.

The remaining four articles in this group evaluated the effectiveness of combined educational and support programs. Goodman and Pynoos (1990) discussed a model telephone support program that considered two components: (a) peer networks, and (b) information provision. The peer network component grouped four to five caregivers who called each other over a 12-week period for informal supportive conversation. The information provision component consisted of 12 taped lectures on topics relevant to Alzheimer's disease (i.e., medical, legal, financial) which the caregivers accessed via phone (one per week). Results indicated that all participants improved on a Subjective Social Support Measure (Zarit, Reever, & Bach-Peterson, 1980) and on knowledge of Alzheimer's disease. The authors noted that one consequence of the network component, however, was a reduction in the utilization of friends and family for emotional support in deference to the support gained from the network caregivers. Conversely, those who listened to the information tapes actually increased their support from friends and family. In light of this, the authors stressed the importance of maintaining existing natural support systems if an alternative support system is offered as part of a caregiver support program. A unique strength of telephone interventions for caregivers is that participants do not have to worry about respite care, transportation, or guilt of leaving their care-recipient, all noted barriers to participation in caregiver programs.

Roberto, Van Amburg, and Orleans (1994) described the development, implementation, and evaluation of the Caregiver Empowerment Project which was designed to enhance churches' roles in supporting caregivers of older adults within their communities. The Project included (a) community education model, (b) social support model, and (c) support group model. The community education model (n = 13) presented workshops about the aging process, financial and legal concerns, emotional aspects, and spiritual needs of caregiving. It also addressed resources and service options. The social support model (n = 13) first provided transportation to the meeting site for those who required it. This model also provided a home delivery shopping service for caregivers who were homebound as well as an interactive resource information forum. The support group model (n = 10) created a formal support group for caregivers which met monthly and was facilitated by two community volunteers. The effects of these three models were evaluated by a focus group made up of volunteer staff from each of the three model groups. The evaluation noted the following specific positive outcomes: (a) the development of new friendships, (b) learning how to identify the needs of older adults and their caregivers, (c) greater awareness of resources, (d) relieving isolation felt by caregivers, and (e) connecting with other programs outside of the immediate community.

Toseland, Labrecque, Goebel, and Whitney (1992) examined the effectiveness of a multi-component group program for spouses of frail aging veterans. The authors used a single blind randomized control group design to evaluate perceived self-efficacy, knowledge and use of community resources, informal social support, and self-ratings of personal change. They also examined measures of burden, coping, depression, stress, anxiety and marital relationships. The intervention group consisted of 8 weekly 2-hour sessions, each of which had four components: (a) support, (b) education and discussion, (c) problem-solving, and (d) stress reduction. The results suggested short term benefits for support group involvement by caregivers. For example, there were significant decreases in stress, severity of problems, and subjective burden. There were significant increases in use of coping strategies, knowledge of community resources, personal changes in ability to cope with the caregiving situation, and perceived independence in marital relationship. The authors recommended that in providing support group programs, professionals need to emphasize to caregivers the importance of maintaining or increasing social support networks.

Hagen, Gallagher, and Simpson (1997) evaluated an education and support program for family caregivers in underserviced communities. The goals of the program were to provide: (a) an opportunity for family and friend caregivers to experience being in a support group, (b) caregivers with experience of being supported in their roles, (c) caregivers with an opportunity to learn more about issues related to caregiving, and (d) caregivers with knowledge about and access to other community services. Each session included an hour of education or discussion on a predetermined topic followed by an hour of an open mutual support group. In-depth interviews conducted three months after the program revealed the following benefits from the program that were related to recreation and social support: (a) "sharing and fellowship," (b) improved communication between caregivers and their family members, (c) increased awareness of community services, (d) increased awareness of own stress and importance of taking care of themselves, (e) increased assertiveness, and (f) being supported in the role of caregiver.

CONCLUSIONS

Upon reviewing the summaries of the studies, several conclusions were evident. First, the combination of education/training and support group in programs showed many benefits for caregivers of older adults. In many cases, there seemed to be similarities and discrepancies between articles that proposed models and programs but did not test them and those articles that did test or measure program effectiveness. For example, a number of articles proposed that education programs would help caregivers balance time and responsibility for their care-recipients and themselves. Rather, based on the programs that were tested, it was the combination of education/training and support groups that demonstrated an effectiveness to this end. In other examples, combined education/training and support groups were not only proposed but actually proven to increase social support for caregivers. Similarly, several of the articles which only proposed programs suggested that the education/training category as well as the combined education/training and support group category would increase caregivers' knowledge and use of community services. No solo education/training program directed at improving caregivers' knowledge and use of community services was tested; however, the combination programs did prove to be effective. Education/training in combination with support groups was associated with an increase in coping skills and a decrease in subjective burden of caregivers. Additionally, one article showed the effectiveness of support groups alone in increasing the caregivers' knowledge and use of community services. Perhaps, the combination of education/training programs with or in the context of support groups is more effective than either type of program alone. This result could be due to the fact that the education component gives the caregivers the information they need, while the support of other caregivers enables them to put that information into action (i.e., using community services and taking care of self).

Second, another proposed benefit of the programs examined was to increase the size of and/or satisfaction with caregivers' social networks. Of the four programs with this focus, two were tested and found to be effective. Additionally, from the articles within this group, Mittleman et al. (1995) found secondary benefits to increasing caregivers' satisfaction with their social networks. They noted, "The effect of an increase in the caregivers' satisfaction with his or her social network, . . . was also associated with a decrease in depression at all follow-ups" (p. 800).

Third, when caregivers made use of respite opportunities, their discretionary time increased. Unfortunately, however, caregivers tended to use this time to run errands or do chores rather than pursue leisure or social experiences. This result, although puzzling, could be due to functional or attitudinal barriers in the caregiver. Either they required a larger block of time to allow for completion of chores before they engage in leisure, or they needed to develop a more positive, guilt-free attitude toward pursuing leisure. In either case, the priority the caregivers place on leisure in their lives seems to be an issue to be considered.

Finally, the purpose of this study was to analyze leisure, recreation, and social programs for caregivers. In the data collection process, however, it became obvious that there were very few programs or interventions for caregivers that used leisure or recreation specifically. Most programs utilized a variety of support group contexts to increase social networks, increase social support, and improve interactions and relationships among families. Perhaps, programmers could consider using recreation and leisure environments as vehicles to achieve these same objectives.

RECOMMENDATIONS

Based on this analysis of recreation/social programs for caregivers of older adults, we offer recommendations for both researchers and practitioners. The first recommendation is directed to both researchers and practitioners. As noted earlier, very few of the implemented or proposed programs were built on or anchored in a theoretical/conceptual framework. For researchers, if research is conducted without a theoretical framework, the generalizability and usability of results will be greatly limited for researchers and practitioners. For practitioners, where programs are successful, without a theoretical/conceptual framework, we cannot say why they are effective. We recommend that designers use a theoretical/conceptual framework to guide them in developing programs such as those described herein. Also, for those programs that are built based on the results of existing literature, it is important to provide a logical and clear link for the reader between the components of the program and the relevant literature. As Miller and Montgomery (1990) noted, "without a comprehensive theory . . . , we can suggest only ad hoc explanations" (p. 90). Therefore, both researchers and practitioners should base their research or programs on clearly identified theoretical/conceptual frameworks.

The second recommendation for practitioners addresses the design of interventions or recreation/leisure programs for caregivers to do on their own (i.e., not facilitated by a professional). The research suggests it is important that such programs be: (a) designed for flexibility of caregiver time and routine, (b) of minimal cost, (c) something that can be done in the home, and (d) built on the existing interests and skills of the caregivers (i.e., Dupuis & Pedlar, 1995; Smith & McCallion, 1997).

Finally, a second recommendation for researchers is to continue to research the efficacy of programs specific to leisure and recreation for caregivers of older adults. Although social and educational programs can provide the knowledge or opportunities for caregivers to pursue their leisure, the lack of proven leisure interventions is notable.

REFERENCES

Barusch, A. S., & Spaid, W. M. (1991). Reducing caregiver burden through short-term training: Evaluation findings from a caregiver support project. *Journal of Gerontological Social Work, 17*(1/2), 7-33.

Bedini, L. A., & Bilbro, C. W. (1991). Caregivers, the hidden victims: Easing caregiver's burden through recreation and leisure services. *Annual in Therapeutic Recreation, 2*, 49-58.

Bedini, L. A., & Phoenix, T. L. (1998). *Addressing leisure barriers for caregivers of older adults: a model leisure wellness program.* Manuscript submitted for publication.

Bedini, L. A., & Guinan, D. M. (1996). The leisure of caregivers of older adults: Implications for CTRS's in non-traditional settings. *Therapeutic Recreation Journal, 30*(4), 274-288.

Berry, G. L., Zarit, S. H., & Rabatin, V. X. (1991). Caregiver activity on respite and nonrespite days: A comparison of two service approaches. *The Gerontologist, 31*, 830-835.

Burks, V. K., Lund, D. A., & Hill, R. D. (1991). Factors associated with attendance at caregiver support group meetings. *Activities, Adaptation & Aging, 15*(3), 93-108.

Cantor, M. H. (1983). Strain among caregivers: A study of experience in the United States. *The Gerontologist, 23*, 597-604.

Coleman, D., & Iso-Ahola, S. E. (1993). Leisure and health: The role of social support and self-determination. *Journal of Leisure Research, 25*, 111-128.

Deimling, G. T. (1991). Respite use and caregiver well-being in families caring for stable and declining AD patients. *Journal of Gerontological Social Work, 18*(1/2), 177-134.

Dupuis, S. L., & Pedlar, A. (1995). Family leisure programs in institutional care settings: Buffering the stress of caregivers. *Therapeutic Recreation Journal, 24*, 184-205.

Enright, R., & Friss, L. (1987). Employed caregivers of brain-impaired adults: An assessment of the dual role. Final report. San Francisco: Family Survival Project.

Fawcett, J., & Downs, F. S. (1986). *The relationship of theory and research.* Norwalk, CT: Appleton-Century-Crofts.

Feinberg, L. F., & Kelly, K. A. (1995). A well-deserved break: Respite programs offered by California's statewide system of caregiver resource centers. *The Gerontologist, 35*, 701-705.

Goodman, C. C. (1991). Perceived social support for caregiving: Measuring the benefit of self-help/support group participation. *Journal of Gerontological Social Work, 16*(3/4), 163-175.

Goodman, C. C., & Pynoos, J. (1990). A model telephone information and support program for caregivers of Alzheimer's patients. *The Gerontologist, 30*(3), 399-404.

Hagan, L. P., Green, F. P., & Starling, S. (1997/98). Addressing stress in caregivers of older adults through leisure education. *Annual in Therapeutic Recreation, 7*, 42-51.

Hagen, B., Gallagher, E. M., & Simpson, S. (1997). Family caregiver education and support programs: Using humanistic approaches to evaluate program effects. *Educational Gerontology, 23*, 129-142.

Hamlet, E., & Read, S. (1990). Caregiver education and support group: A hospital based group experience. *Journal of Gerontological Social Work, 15*(1/2), 75-88.

Henderson, K. A. (1991). *Dimensions of choice: A qualitative approach to recreation, parks, and leisure research.* State College, PA: Venture, Inc.

Hughes, S., & Keller, M. J. (1992). Leisure education: A coping strategy for family caregivers. *Journal of Gerontological Social Work, 19*(1), 155-128.

Jackson, G. B. (1980). Methods for integrative reviews. *Review of Educational Research, 50*(3), 438-460.

Jaloweic, A., Murphy, S., & Powers, M. (1984). Psychometric assessment of the Jaloweic coping scale. *Nursing Research, 33*(3), 157-161.

Keller, M. J., & Hughes, S. (1991). The role of leisure education with family caregivers of persons with Alzheimer's Disease and related disorders. *Annual in Therapeutic Recreation, 2*, 1-7.

Lieberman, M. S. (1979). Help seeking and self-help groups (pp. 116-149). In M. A. Lieberman, L. D. Borman, & Associates (Eds.). *Self-help groups for coping with crisis.* San Francisco: Jossey-Bass.

Lund, D. A., Hill, R. D., Caserta, M. S., & Wright, S. D. (1995). Video Respite: An innovative resource for family, professional caregivers, and persons with dementia. *The Gerontologist, 35*, 683-687.

McCallion, P., & Toseland, R. W. (1995). Supportive group interventions with caregivers of frail older adults. *Social Work with Groups, 18*(1), 11-25.

Miller, B., & Montgomery, A. (1990). Family caregivers and limitations in social activities. *Research on Aging, 12*(1), 72-93.

Mittelman, M. S., Ferris, S. H., Shulman, E., Steinberg, G., Ambinder, A., Mackell, J. A., & Cohen, J. (1995). A comprehensive support program: Effect on depression in spouse-caregivers of AD patients. *The Gerontologist, 35*, 792-802.

Montgomery, R., & Borgatta, E. (1986, November). *Creation of burden scales.* Paper presented at the 38th Annual Scientific Meeting of the Gerontological Society of America, New Orleans.

Moss, M. S., & Lawton, M. P. (1982). Time budgets of older people: A window on four life-styles. *Journal of Gerontology, 37*(1), 115-123.

Moss, M. S., Lawton, M. P., Kleban, M. H., & Duhamel, L. (1993). Time use of caregivers of impaired elders before and after institutionalization. *Journal of Gerontology: Social Sciences, 48*, S102-S111.

Noelker, L., & Bass, D. (1989). Home care for elderly persons: Linkages between formal and informal caregivers. *Journal of Gerontology, 44*, S63-S72.

Peterson, C. A., & Gunn, S. L. (1984). *Therapeutic Recreation Program Design.* Englewood Cliffs, NJ: Prentice-Hall.

Poulshock, S. W., & Deimling, G. T. (1984). Families caring for elders in residence: Issues in the measurement of burden. *Journal of Gerontology, 39*, 230-239.

Roberto, K. A., Amburg, S. V., & Orleans, M. (1994). The caregiver empowerment project: Developing programs within rural communities. *Activities, Adaptation & Aging, 18*(2), 1-12.

Schopler, J. H., & Galinsky, M. J. (1983). Support groups as open systems: A model for practice and research. *Health and Social Work, 18*, 195-207.

Smith, D. J., & McCallion, P. (1997). Alleviating stress of family caregivers of frail elders using horticultural therapy. *Activities, Adaptation & Aging, 22*(1/2), 93-105.

Smyth, K. A., & Harris, P. B. (1993). Using telecomputing to provide information and support to caregivers of persons with dementia. *The Gerontologist, 33*, 123-127.

Sneh, N., & Tristan, J. (1991). Plant material arrangements in therapy. *Journal of Therapeutic Horticulture, 6*, 16-20.

Stokes, J. P. (1983). Predicting satisfaction with social support from social network structure. *American Journal of Community Psychology, 11*, 141-152.

Thompson, E. H., Futterman, A. M., Gallagher-Thompson, D., Rose, J. M., & Lovett, S. B. (1993). Social support and caregiving burden in family caregivers of frail elders. *Journal of Gerontology: Social Sciences, 48*, S245-S254.

Toseland, R. W., Labrecque, M. S., Goebel, S. T., & Whitney, M. H. (1992). An evaluation of a group program for spouses of frail elderly veterans. *The Gerontologist, 32*, 382-390.

Williams, S. (1989). Evaluation of a horticulture therapy program in a short-term psychiatric ward. *Journal of Therapeutic Horticulture, 4*, 29-38.

Wilson, V. (1990). The consequences of elderly wives caring for disabled husbands: Implications for practice. *Social Work, 35*(5).

Wood, V., Wiley, M. L., & Sheafor, G. (1969). An analysis of short self-report measure of life satisfaction: Correlation and rater judgments. *Journal of Gerontology, 24*, 465-469.

Zarit, S. R., Reever, K. E., & Bach-Peterson, J. (1980). Relatives of impaired elderly: Correlates of feelings of burden. *The Gerontologist, 20*, 651-656.

Family Obligation, Caregiving, and Loss of Leisure: The Experiences of Three Caregivers

Nancy Brattain Rogers

SUMMARY. This article presents in-depth case studies of three care-givers of older husbands with dementia. The cases highlight the women's rationale behind sacrificing leisure in order to provide better care. A relationship between a strong sense of family obligation and sacrifice of leisure is explored. *[Article copies available for a fee from The Haworth Document Delivery Service: 1-800-342-9678. E-mail address: getinfo@haworthpressinc.com <Website: http://www.haworthpressinc.com>]*

KEYWORDS. Caregiving, leisure, respite

Many older adults in the U.S. will require assistance with activities of daily living for a period ranging from a few months to several years prior to death (Ferrini & Ferrini, 1993). Female family members typically provide such assistance in the home of either the caregiver or care recipient (Hartman, 1990). Wives provide the majority of care to older men and approximately 23% of all care given to older adults irrespective of relationships (Stone, Cafferata, & Sangl, 1987). Adult daughters provide 29% of care to older adults and husbands provide 13% of care. Other relatives and formal service providers provide the remaining care.

Nancy Brattain Rogers, PhD, is Assistant Professor, Recreation and Sport Management, Indiana State University, Terre Haute, IN 47805 (E-mail: rcrogers@scifac.indstate.edu).

[Haworth co-indexing entry note]: "Family Obligation, Caregiving, and Loss of Leisure: The Experiences of Three Caregivers." Rogers, Nancy Brattain. Co-published simultaneously in *Activities, Adaptation & Aging* (The Haworth Press, Inc.) Vol. 24, No. 2, 1999, pp. 35-49; and: *Caregiving-Leisure and Aging* (ed: M. Jean Keller) The Haworth Press, Inc., 1999, pp. 35-49. Single or multiple copies of this article are available for a fee from The Haworth Document Delivery Service [1-800-342-9678, 9:00 a.m. - 5:00 p.m. (EST). E-mail address: getinfo@haworthpressinc.com].

The impact of caregiving on many facets of women's lives has been well-documented (Hartman, 1990; Sommers, 1985). Increased stress, disease, social isolation, and a reduction in time for oneself are common consequences of caregiving. Although a reduction in free time, social networks, and other leisure-related factors are well documented in the lives of caregivers, there is a dearth of literature that describes the impact of caregiving on leisure in detail. The intent of this study is to explore the perspectives of leisure of three caregiving wives who have withdrawn from leisure in conjunction with providing care to their husbands.

WHY WOMEN GIVE CARE

Writings about women's role as caregivers have been common since the early 19th century. Between 1820 and 1865 popular writers frequently discussed women's "special sphere" which was their ability to respond to the needs of others (Abel, 1994). Diaries and journals written by women in this period indicated that caregiving was a common experience (Abel). As with caregivers today, 18th century women thought their care was superior to care provided by others. Infrequent contact with and mistrust of physicians, as well as the view of hospitals as custodial institutions for the poor, contributed to women's role as caregivers. In the late 19th century and early 20th century older adults began placing substantial caregiving burdens on women (Abel, 1991). Prior to this time, most people died of acute infectious diseases before they reached what now is considered old age.

The majority of families that provide care believe the quality of care they provide is preferable to institutional care and institutional care should be utilized as a last resort (Aronson, 1992; Barusch, 1991). Lewis and Meredith (1988) found in a qualitative study of caregiving daughters that formal services often are not utilized due to fear that they are not reliable. McKinlay, Crawford, and Tennestedt (1995) found caregivers believe the positive aspects of caregiving outweigh the negative aspects.

NEGATIVE EFFECTS OF CAREGIVING

Tremendous time constraints impact the lives of most caregivers. Many caregivers have reported that they feel constantly responsible for the welfare of the care recipient (Lewis & Meredith, 1988). Wilson (1990) determined that 85% of wife caregivers found the emotional and physical strain of caregiving was exhausting and frustrating. It is apparently very difficult for caregivers to plan for future activities because they cannot predict the future health status of the person receiving care (Abel, 1991). The uncertainty of how long care will continue also constrains caregivers' ability to plan for the future (Lewis & Meredith, 1988).

Guilt is a common feeling that contributes to caregivers' inability to take time away from caregiving responsibilities (Aronson, 1992; Green, Hebron, & Woodward, 1987). Sommers and Shields (1987) found that guilt was a prominent feeling among caregivers. The women felt social pressure to be good caregivers and did not believe they were meeting those expectations. Perkinson (1995) found that caregivers valued autonomy and felt it was inappropriate to ask others for help.

Caregivers experience lower life satisfaction, increased depression, and lower health status in comparison to the general older population (Mohide et al., 1990). Staight and Harvey (1990) found that 52% of primary caregivers contacted through private and public home health service agencies were not very satisfied with their lives. Their research also indicated that primary and secondary caregivers were more lonely and depressed than elderly non-caregivers. The life satisfaction scores for a sample of caregiving wives tested by Wilson (1990) were significantly lower than those of a national sample of older adults. Mui (1995) found that poorer health status of wife caregivers was predicted by depression of the care recipient. Furthermore, health status and functional status were affected by care recipients' unmet needs. These findings were attributed to the tendency of women to feel responsible for the well being of family members.

CAREGIVING AS A CONSTRAINT TO LEISURE

Research has consistently indicated that satisfaction with one's leisure is highly correlated to overall life satisfaction in middle and late adulthood (Kelly, Steinkamp, & Kelly, 1986; Riddick, 1985; Riddick & Daniel, 1984). Unfortunately, leisure is not a reality for many caregivers.

The sacrifice of leisure to spend time fulfilling caregiving demands has been reported by women throughout the past two centuries (Abel, 1991; Aronson, 1992). Women in the 19th century complained in their journals that caregiving kept them from attending church or social activities (Abel, 1991). In a comparison study of primary and secondary wife caregivers, Staight and Harvey (1990) found that primary caregivers had significantly less free time than secondary caregivers. Commissaris et al. (1995) found that caregivers experienced social isolation due to decreased contact with family and friends. Wilson (1990) concluded that 74% of caregiving wives believed that caregiving responsibilities had negatively affected their social activities. These negative effects included limited contacts and visits with friends and family, social isolation, and elimination of opportunities to volunteer and participate in other social activities.

Keller and Tu (1994) investigated the relationship between leisure and perceived burden of spouse caregivers of persons with Alzheimer's disease. Caregivers in this study reported a 50% reduction in leisure activities since assuming caregiving responsibilities. Self-reported health was the most significant variable that entered into the regression analysis of leisure satisfaction. A number of other variables correlated with caregivers' self-reported health status included: amount of leisure time, leisure satisfaction, perceived freedom in leisure, leisure barriers, and perceived burden. The variables that explained the majority of perceived burden included caregivers' health, amount of help from friends and family, and caregiving hours per day. Amount of help also related to leisure satisfaction, perceived freedom in leisure, leisure barriers, and perceived burden.

DEFINING LEISURE FOR CAREGIVERS

In the past decade, some feminist researchers (Bella, 1989; Henderson et al., 1989) have suggested that common definitions of leisure are inadequate for explaining women's leisure. The previous definitions, which defined leisure as freedom from obligation, are very difficult to apply to caregivers. The constant sense of responsibility that women report feeling, in addition to the burden and guilt, make it very unlikely that these women feel free from their caregiving obligations. If these women truly do not experience freedom, then it could be assumed, based on the definition of leisure as freedom, those caregivers do not experience leisure. It also is possible that the leisure as freedom definition is incomplete or inappropriate for application to female caregivers. If the leisure as freedom definition is not applicable, then it is possible that leisure does have meaning for caregivers but prior studies have not discovered that meaning.

Pruette (1972) suggested that the irregularity and uncertainty of women's work, including caregiving, make it difficult for women to plan for leisure. In a study of the leisure of 1610 women in England, Green et al. (1987) stated, " . . . the amorphous nature of women's unpaid domestic work as carers makes it hard to identify time which is unambiguously 'free' for leisure" (p. 10). A rethinking of traditional views of leisure may be in order to understand the experiences of wife caregivers.

METHOD

The case studies of three caregiving wives are presented in this study. The participants were selected from a larger sample of caregivers from an on-going project that explored the relationship between leisure and caregiving (Rogers, 1995). The three caregivers in this study were selected for the sample due to their sacrifice of most or all leisure and social activities during the period they were providing care and the dominance of the caregiving role in their lives.

Data were collected through in-depth interviews conducted at participants' homes. Interviews ranged in length from 90 to 150 minutes. An unstructured, open-ended ethnographic interview format was utilized (Fontana & Frey, 1994). Interview questions were quite broad in nature and were developed to facilitate dialogue regarding the caregiver's leisure, barriers to leisure, and the impact of caregiving on leisure. The interviews began with questions designed to obtain the basic details of the caregiving situation: the nature of the husband's disability, the extent of care required, the length of time the participant had provided care, the history of the progression of the husband's disease, and his prognosis for the future. Basic demographic information was also obtained including the age of the participants and their husbands, the length of their marriages, number of children, length of time in their residences, and the work histories of the participants and their husbands. After the basic information was obtained, broad questions were utilized to facilitate dialogue regarding the caregiver's leisure and the impact of caregiving on leisure. It was common for the women to begin talking about their frustrations with caregiving before the first question was asked.

The interviews were audiotaped and transcribed in entirety. I then began analyzing the transcripts according to the constant comparative method outlined by Strauss and Corbin (1990). Data analysis began upon completion of the first transcript.

Memo writing was used throughout data analysis to identify potential problems, question the development of the study, and express discovery of emerging patterns (Glesne & Peshkin, 1992). Some of the topics expressed in the memos included: ideas about the relationship between life history and leisure participation, surprise at the active social life of some of the integrated caregivers, and the need for developing a diverse sample.

In addition to memos, accounts of initial contacts and interviews (field notes) were kept in a reflexive journal. I recorded impressions of the participants, descriptions of their homes, accounts of my initial contact with the participants, and other important information. The journal was referred to throughout data analysis to cross-validate the emergent framework.

A member check was conducted to confirm that the findings represented the thoughts of the participants (Lincoln & Guba, 1985). Member checking was accomplished by providing findings and supportive evidence to participants for their review. All of the participants were mailed a case report after their interview with a request to correct or amend the findings. Thirteen of the participants returned the reports. One participant also called me after the interview to talk about her situation.

FINDINGS

During the course of the original study it became clear that although caregiving was an overwhelming barrier to leisure, some of the women could find time for leisure (Rogers, 1995). It also became clear that the severity of the husbands' disabilities or diseases and the amount of care required could not explain whether or not the women pursued leisure. This finding is congruent with research (Aneshensel, Pearlin, & Schuler, 1993; Phillips et al., 1995; Pruchno et al., 1990; Zarit, Todd, & Zarit, 1986) that indicated that the severity of the patient's illness is not a reliable predictor of caregiver burden and depression. Gubrium's (1991) statement about caregiving that "nothing is inevitable" (p. 53) implied that caregiving is experienced differently by every woman. The original study supports that finding. The factor that was most important in predicting leisure behavior was the caregiver's beliefs about the role of caregiving and how much of their identity was consumed by that role. The ability of the women to define themselves in ways that expanded beyond the caregiving role was essential for leisure. The women in this study did not identify themselves beyond the context of the caregiving relationship.

The most dominant characteristic of the caregivers was their strong family orientation. The participants placed so much importance on the caregiving that other non-family related roles had become irrelevant. Although some of the women had other roles (employee, volunteer, etc.) prior to the onset of caregiving, these roles were not highly valued and were relinquished as the demands of caregiving increased. One participant described how she had not developed strong social ties outside of the family.

> I guess we kind of lived for ourselves, our work, and our kids–getting them through school and on their way. (P8-219-5)

During later life, the role of mother became less important and the women spent increasing time and energy on sharing the retirement years with their husbands. The strong orientation toward identifying oneself as a part of a couple, rather than an individual, explains the difficulty these caregivers experienced in regards to finding leisure. One participant indicated, "Why would I go out if I can't go with him?" Her view was representative of all the participants.

Although the preference of the participants for couple leisure helps explain the caregivers' abandonment of leisure, the relationship between the caregivers' strong family orientation and the dissolution of leisure is more complex. The following case studies illustrate how overwhelming family orientation contributes to the dissolution of leisure.

Denial of the Current Caregiving Situation and Avoidance of the Future: The Case of Mary

Mary was 76 years old and had been married to her 79 year-old husband, Bill, for 59 years. Bill was a deliveryman until he retired at age 65. Mary retired from domestic work at age 68. The couple had lived for over 40 years in a small bungalow in a Midwestern community of 60,000 residents.

Bill was diagnosed with Alzheimer's disease and required 24-hour care. He could not be left alone for any length of time due to his tendency to engage in potentially harmful behavior. When the weather was warm he often escaped from the house and wandered through the neighborhood. Bill and Mary's son had insisted that Mary give up her car due to his concern that Bill would get the keys and try to drive. Mary complied and was currently without transportation, in spite of the fact that she still had her license. Bill no longer recognized Mary. He often was uncooperative and physically abusive. Recently, he had started urinating in inappropriate places including the closet and the sink. Mary had a difficult time acknowledging the changes in her husband's behavior. Comments regarding Bill's behavior were typically qualified with statements about what a good man he was.

> . . . if he'd just be cooperative. He's such a good man. But, he'll fight with me, I don't know. . . He would get so upset. He doesn't listen anymore.

> It takes me a long time to talk to him and a lot of time in the mornings he doesn't want to open his eyes while he's sitting at the table. . . . It's just not easy. . . He's always been so cooperative and such a good husband.

> He's gone to the bathroom before he gets his clothes off. I went in there [bedroom] one day and he had half his clothes off the hangers. He's always worked hard all of his life.

Mary constantly referred to the past as a method of rationalizing the current situation.

In spite of the rapid decline in Bill's functional ability over a four-year period and his need for constant attention, Mary refused to acknowledge that the caregiving situation was changing and becoming unmanageable without additional assistance.

> Then three times he couldn't wait till I got his pants down for him to use the bathroom and he wet his pants. I had to change his clothes. I hope it doesn't continue like that. I hope he gets better.

In spite of the doctor's indication that Bill was not going to get better, Mary was hopeful that he would improve.

In light of Bill's declining functional status, the doctor, family and friends pressured Mary to consider long-term care. She was resistant.

> He's always had a fear of nursing homes. I said, "Honey, as long as I'm on my two feet and I can, I'll take care of you no matter what the load." The nurse told me I shouldn't have told him that because there might be a time that I might have to go or something . . . I was told by some of them at the nursing home that if you didn't cooperate, they'd tie you to the bed.

Mary had reached the point where she could not manage her husband's behavior, but she was not willing to acknowledge that additional care was required, especially if that meant breaking a promise to her husband.

Finally, Mary was not making plans for the future. She admitted that she actively avoided thinking about the future.

> I should try to think about it more, but I try not to think about it because it upsets me. I just try to think well maybe something good will happen. Maybe they'll find a way to make him better. Then I try not to think. I've always said I didn't want my children to be bothered with me when I got old and couldn't take care of myself. It upsets them if I mention anything to them about it. I say, "I don't want you to take care of me. If I have to go to a nursing home, I just want you to come and see me." Because I don't want to interfere with their lives.

This statement was typical of Mary's feelings about and interactions with her family. Although Mary felt obligated to provide all of her husband's care, she did not want to place the same burden on her children. Her primary concern was for doing what was best for her family–regardless of the sacrifice.

Guilt and Caregiving: The Case of Alice

Alice and John were 73 years old and had been married for 49 years. The couple had retired from ownership of a small business 12 years prior to the interview. They lived in a condominium that they purchased two years after their retirement. Their home was located in a Midwestern community of 20,000 residents.

John's health problems stemmed from his diabetes. He had substantial visual impairment and sensory loss in his lower legs. As a result, his balance was very poor and he frequently fell. John used a walker in the house, but believed that a walker was too humiliating to use in public. When Alice and John went out, he walked with a cane and leaned on his wife. In addition to the sensory loss in his legs, John could no longer independently dress or use the toilet.

Although the physical demands of caring for John were somewhat rigorous, the greatest stress in Alice's life came from John's behavior. He was demanding and manipulative toward his wife. Alice was afraid to confront his behavior because she felt it was her responsibility to keep him in "good spirits." When John became angry with Alice she felt guilty about not being a good wife and caregiver. John's control over the household was evident. He refused to let his wife participate in this interview on her own. He interrupted her and corrected her answers. She was not able to honestly respond to questions about the caregiving situation until she took me on a tour of the house and we were alone in the basement.

John frequently experienced what Alice called "panic attacks" during the early hours of the morning. The behavior that followed each "panic attack" illustrates John's manipulation and Alice's guilt. During each attack, John insisted that Alice get him out of bed and take him for a ride.

> Then he wants to ride, so we go through the process of getting dressed, we go for a ride, maybe I'm just ready to go to bed. Maybe it's two in the morning, the other morning it was four o'clock and we went for a ride. Now he has what he calls a happy pill. I told the doctor I had to have something. Because he wants the windows open. He wants the doors open. He's sort of half-frantic. So we take a ride. Go ever so slowly. . . Sometimes it's an hour and a half, sometimes it's two hours.

Although John's doctor discouraged Alice from complying with his demands for early morning car rides, she felt too guilty about telling her husband no.

> The doctor gave him some happy pills, but he says he won't take them and become an addict. Sometimes he says he'd be better off dead. I'm afraid he might do something. It's better to keep him happy.

John frequently threatened suicide when his wife did not comply with his wishes.

During Alice's tour of the house she confided that caring for her husband was a burden. Like Mary, Alice had promised her husband she would take care of him regardless of the circumstances. Alice was frustrated by her husband's manipulation, but was unwilling to challenge his demands. She described how John would suggest that Alice take a few hours to paint in the basement. As soon as she set up her easel and got out her paints, he would call for her. If she tried to return to painting, he would threaten to harm himself. The couple did not seek outside counseling or support. Alice believed that her husband's happiness was her responsibility. If John was not happy, then she must not be providing adequate care.

Turning Down Help: The Case of Ruth

Ruth was 70 years old and had been married to 71 year-old Norm for 51 years. Ruth retired from a clerk's position in a small business 5 years prior to the interview. Norm has been retired from store management for 20 years. He was diagnosed with scleroderma 30 years prior to the interview. Ruth had been providing full-time care for the past 5 years. Norm had no sensation in his feet and could not walk. The disease also had compromised his lung capacity. At the time of the interview, Norm had a number of skin ulcers that were not healing.

Ruth managed all of the household labor. She cooked, cleaned, did the laundry, shopped, and did the yard work. In addition to household labor, she dressed and bathed her husband, assisted with toileting, and bandaged his ulcers several times a day. She left the house twice a week for 30 minutes to go to the grocery store.

Norm's doctor had attempted to arrange home health services through a local service provider. A social worker had visited Ruth and Norm, but was unsuccessful in convincing Ruth that she should take advantage of services. Ruth made the following response when asked why she did not use respite services:

> We worked like dogs all our life. We retired. And we don't ask much out of life. But I just wish we would have been able to go once in a while. Just go out and eat where one of us wouldn't have to push the other one in a wheelchair. Not much, I don't ask for. But, you know as far as people calling here and saying, "Well do you want to go to a movie or something?" I'll say, "No, I don't want to go to the movie," cause we always went together. I don't enjoy it.

Ruth also balked at suggestions from her family that she should get out more.

> I just told my sister. I said, "I'm gonna tell you something. Your husbands can walk in with you." They've both got their second husbands, and I'm fighting like hell to keep my first one with me and I said, "You just try pushing yours in there in a wheelchair and see how you do."

Respite was clearly not desirable since any outings would not include Norm.

Ruth had an adult daughter living in the same town. The daughter frequently offered assistance with Norm's care, but Ruth refused her offers. Ruth offered the following rationalization:

> She just went through a pretty nasty divorce. She works at a radio station and keeps pretty busy. She's got kids and grandkids living with her. If I really needed her, she'd be here. But as far as her running out here, she's got too much to do. She shouldn't have to worry about us.

Ruth was like Alice. She felt responsible for keeping her husband and her children happy. She would not accept offers of assistance from her daughter, because there might be negative consequences for her daughter. It was clear to Ruth that she should bear the burden of caregiving alone.

CONCLUSION

The preceding account of caregivers' lives presents a complex picture of leisure and caregiving. For the women in this study, leisure entitlement is an intractable concept. The women's overwhelming sense of obligation to their husbands and family made leisure, in effect, meaningless and their social lives and leisure dissolved. Regardless of how sense of obligation to family members was manifested, these caregivers were totally committed to selflessly doing what was best for the family.

Prior to the onset of the husband's illness, leisure had meant the opportunity to foster relationships with husbands and other family members. As a consequence, leisure for the women in this study must be conceptualized within the context of relationships. This conceptualization requires a revision of previous notions of leisure as freedom (Ibrahim, 1991; Kraus, 1990; Neulinger, 1974). It is not entirely inappropriate to discard the notion of freedom, however the use of freedom to describe caregiver leisure should be used in the context of freedom to pursue relationships rather than freedom from obligation. From this perspective of leisure, the caregivers were free from some types of obligations related to domestic labor or employment during leisure, however their sense of obligation to family was a very important part of their leisure. If obligations to family could not be met during leisure, the women would abandon leisure.

Implications for Practice

The results of this study and others indicate that there is no simple, systematic method of determining how wives will react to the caregiving situation.

Measures of time spent caring and the severity of the husbands' disabilities are not sufficient to predict caregiver burden and loss of leisure. An approach that requires individual assessment of each caregiver seems more appropriate. The results of previous intervention studies and the comments of women in this study indicate a new approach to serving caregivers is in order. Caregiver education programs, home health services, respite, and other support programs cannot be effective with women who will not relinquish care of their husbands to help themselves. If behavior change is to occur, extensive support, including counseling, may be necessary. Support programs also may be more successful if service providers can establish a strong link between taking time for oneself and improving one's ability to care. Caregivers with a strong family orientation are unlikely to be convinced that leisure is important simply because it is good for them.

Perhaps the most successful solution, and also the most difficult, to improving the lives of caregivers is to change women's perceptions of themselves and their roles in life. Women's ability and desire to nurture and care for their families should not be discouraged; however, this aspect of their lives should not always dominate. Women may find more satisfaction with their lives if they develop a variety of roles that meet their needs for affiliation and self-worth. Changing the perceptions of women, or society, is not easy. The caregivers in this study held their views about the centrality of the family all of their lives. It is unlikely that those beliefs will change easily. Gilligan and her colleagues (Gilligan, Lyons, & Hanmer, 1990) found that many girls become complacent during adolescence in order to be more accommodating and pleasing to others. It seems likely that the ethic of care that drives older caregivers starts to develop during these adolescent years. As a consequence, an effective approach to helping older women may be to encourage teachers, recreation programmers, coaches, parents, and other adults who work with children to work with girls and young women to help them develop an integrated lifestyle. For example, there is clear evidence that girls who participate in organized sports have higher self-esteem and become sexually active at a later age. These characteristics in adolescence indicate development of a holistic or integrated sense of self. As a consequence, continued and increased support of girls' athletic programs may improve the lives of women throughout adulthood. Henderson and her colleagues (Henderson, Bialeschki, Shaw, & Freysinger, 1996) concluded that girls who participate in demanding leisure activities that require effort and concentration are likely to be happier, more satisfied adults. Adults can facilitate involvement in challenging leisure activities by providing athletic, art, music, reading and other types of programs as an alternative to socializing, going to the mall, or engaging in other diversionary activities. Leisure education or lifestyle education programs also should be considered. For example, physical educators can teach girls the lifelong benefits of participating in fitness activity. Music and art educators can teach parents the cognitive and developmental benefits of participation in their programs. The key is to view women in the context of a lifetime of social interaction. Women who engage in a lifetime of social relationships that encourage independence and individuality may be better equipped to handle the strenuous demands of caregiving that often accompany later life.

REFERENCES

Abel, E. (1991). *Who cares for the elderly? Public policy and the experiences of adult daughters.* Philadelphia:Temple University Press.

Abel, E.K. (1994). Historical perspectives on caregiving: Documenting women's experiences, in J.F. Gubrium & A. Sankar (Eds.), *Qualitative methods in aging.* Newbury Park, CA: Sage Publications, pp. 227-242.

Aneshensel, C.S., Pearlin, L.I., and Schuler, R.N. (1993, March). Stress, role captivity, and the cessation of caregiving. *Journal of Health and Social Behavior, 34,* 54-70.

Aronson, J. (1992). Women's sense of responsibility for the care of old people: But who else is going to do it?, *Gender and Society,* 6(1), 8-29.

Barusch, A.S. (1991). *Elder care: Family training and support.* Newbury Park, CA: Sage Publications.

Bella, L. (1989). Women and leisure: Beyond androcentrism. *Understanding leisure and recreation: Mapping the past, charting the future.* State College, PA: Venture Publishing, pp. 151-180.

Commissaris, C.J.A.M., Jolles, J., Verhey, F.R.J., & Kok, G.J. (1995). Problems of caregiving spouses with dementia. *Patient Education and Counseling, 25,* 143-149.

Ferrini, A.F., & Ferrini, R.L. (1993). *Health in the later years.* (2nd ed.). Dubuque, IA: William Brown Communications, Inc.

Gilligan, C., Lyons, N.P., & Hamner, (1990). *Making connections: The relational worlds of adolescent girls at Emma Willard school.* Cambridge, MA: Harvard University Press.

Glesne, C., & Peshkin, A. (1992). *Becoming qualitative researchers: An introduction.* White Plains, NY: Longman Publishing Group.

Green, E., Hebron, S., & Woodward, D. (1987). Leisure and gender: A study of Sheffield women's leisure experiences. Sheffield, UK: The Sports Council and Economic and Social Research Council.

Gubrium, J.F. (1991). *The mosaic of care.* New York: Springer Publishing Company.

Hartman, A. (1990). Aging as a feminist issue. *Social Work,* 35(5), 387-388.

Henderson, K., Bialeschki, M.D., Shaw, S.M., & Freysinger, V.J. (1996). *Both gains and gaps: A feminist perspective of women's leisure.* State College, PA: Venture Publishing.

Henderson, K., Bialeschki, M.D., Shaw, S.M., & Freysinger, V.J. (1989). *A leisure of one's own: A feminist perspective on women's leisure.* State College, PA: Venture Publishing.

Ibrahim, H. (1991). *Leisure and society: A comparative approach.* Dubuque, IA: William C. Brown Publishers.

Keller, M.J., & Tu, S.F. (1994, October). The relationships between leisure and perceived burden of spouse caregivers of persons with Alzheimer's disease. Paper presented at the annual meeting of the National Recreation and Park Association.

Kelly, J.R., Steinkamp, M.W., & Kelly, J.R. (1986). Later life leisure: How they play in Peoria. *The Gerontologist, 26*(5), 531-537.

Lewis, J., and Meredith, B. (1988). *Daughters who care: Daughters caring for mother at home.* New York: Routledge.

Lincoln, Y.S., & Guba, E.G. (1985). *Naturalistic inquiry.* Newbury Park, CA: Sage Publications.

McKinlay, J.B., Crawford, S.L. & Tennestedt, S.L. (1995). The everyday impacts of providing informal care to dependent elders and their consequences for the care recipients. *Journal of Aging and Health,* (4), 497-528.

Mohide, A., Pringle, D., Streiner, D., Gilbert, J., Muir, G., & Tew, M. (1990). A randomized trial of family caregiver support in the home management of dementia. *Journal of the American Geriatrics Society, 38*(7), 446-454.

Mui, A.C. (1995). Perceived health and functional status among spouse caregivers of frail older persons. *Journal of Aging and Health, 7*(2), 283-300.

Neulinger, J. (1974). *The psychology of leisure.* Springfield, IL: Charles C. Thomas, Publisher.

Perkinson, M.A. (1995). Socialization to the family caregiving role within a continuing care retirement community. *Medical Anthropology, 16,* 249-267.

Phillips, L.R., Morrison, E., Steffl, B., Chae, Y.M., Cromwell, S.L., & Russell, C.K. (1995). Effects of the situational context and interactional process on the quality of family caregiving. *Research in Nursing and Health, 18,* 205-216.

Pruchno, R.A., Kleban, M.H., Michael, E., & Dempsey, N.P. (1990). Mental and physical health of caregiving spouses: Development of a causal model. *Journals of Gerontology, 45,*(5) P192-199.

Pruette, L. (1972). *Women and leisure: A study of social waste.* New York: Arno Press.

Riddick, C. (1985). Life satisfaction determinants of older males and females. *Leisure Sciences, 1*(1), 47-63.

Riddick, C.C., & Daniel, S.N. (1984). The relative contribution of leisure activities and other factors to the mental health of older women. *Journal of Leisure Research, 16,* (2), 136-148.

Rogers, N.B. (1995). The meaning of leisure from the perspective of wife caregivers of older husbands. Indiana University. Unpublished doctoral dissertation.

Sommers, T. (1985). Caregiving: A woman's issue, *Generations, 10,* (1), 9-13.

Sommers, T., & Shields, L. (1987). *Women who take care: The consequences of caregiving in today's society.* Gainesville, FL: Triad Publishing Co.

Staight, P.R., & Harvey, S.M. (1990). Caregiver burden: A comparison between elderly women as primary and secondary caregivers for their spouses. *Journal of Gerontological Social Work, 15*(1/2), 89-101.

Stone, R., Cafferata, G.L., & Sangl, J. (1987). Caregivers of the frail elderly: A national profile. *The Gerontologist, 27*(5), 485-506.

Strauss, A., & Corbin, J. (1990). *Basis of qualitative research: Grounded theory procedures and techniques.* Newbury Park, CA: Sage Publications.

Wilson, V. (1990). The consequences of elderly wives caring for disabled husbands: Implications for practice. *Social Work, 35,*(5), 417-421.

Zarit, S.H., Todd, P.A., & Zarit, J.M. (1986). Subjective burden of husbands and wives as caregivers: A longitudinal study. *The Gerontologist, 26*(3), 260-266.

Rural vs. Urban Caregivers of Older Adults with Probable Alzheimer's Disease: Perceptions Regarding Daily Living and Recreation Needs

Linda L. Buettner
Sarah Langrish

SUMMARY. A survey of 76 caregivers of individuals with probable Alzheimer's disease was completed over a 2 1/2 year period through the Alzheimer's Disease Assistance Center at Binghamton University. The survey was used to assess educational and support needs for the families in rural and urban settings. The analysis of the data showed that rural caregivers and care receivers were significantly older, and used fewer services than urban families. Caregivers in both settings were very interested in learning about how to provide activities and recreation for their family member with Alzheimer's disease. Over 90% of rural families expressed an interest in learning new ways to keep their family member busy with meaningful activities in and out of the home. *[Article copies available for a fee from The Haworth Document Delivery Service: 1-800-342-9678. E-mail address: getinfo@haworthpressinc.com <Website: http://www.haworthpressinc.com>]*

KEYWORDS. Alzheimer's disease, recreation, community-based services, rural caregivers

---

Linda L. Buettner, CTRS, PhD, is Assistant Professor, Decker School of Nursing, Binghamton University, Binghamton, NY 13902-6000.

Sarah Langrish, RN, is a graduate student, Decker School of Nursing, Family Nurse Practitioner Program.

[Haworth co-indexing entry note]: "Rural vs. Urban Caregivers of Older Adults with Probable Alzheimer's Disease: Perceptions Regarding Daily Living and Recreation Needs." Buettner, Linda L., and Sarah Langrish. Co-published simultaneously in *Activities, Adaptation & Aging* (The Haworth Press, Inc.) Vol. 24, No. 2, 1999, pp. 51-65; and: *Caregiving-Leisure and Aging* (ed: M. Jean Keller) The Haworth Press, Inc., 1999, pp. 51-65. Single or multiple copies of this article are available for a fee from The Haworth Document Delivery Service [1-800-342-9678, 9:00 a.m. - 5:00 p.m. (EST). E-mail address: getinfo@haworthpressinc.com].

Alzheimer's disease (AD) is a long lasting and ultimately debilitating illness that currently affects over four million Americans (Evans, 1990). The disease progresses in stages, gradually destroying short-term memory, judgment, language, and reasoning abilities. The individual eventually loses the ability to perform such routine tasks as feeding, dressing, bathing, toileting, and moving around. In addition, the person experiences a loss of meaningful activity in his or her life and may become unsafe due to falls or environmental hazards (Buettner & Waitkavitz, 1998). Caring for individuals with Alzheimer's disease is a difficult and emotionally draining task for family members, who often assume sole responsibility of their loved ones prior to institutionalization (Zarit, Orr, & Zarit, 1985). As the nation's population ages, the numbers affected will continue to grow. With no cure on the horizon, it is important that we recognize the needs of the family with Alzheimer's in both the rural and urban setting to better manage or prevent excessive disability and premature placement.

In the tri-county area of the Southern Tier of New York served by the Decker School of Nursing's Alzheimer's Disease Assistance Center (ADAC), there are 47,107 individuals over the age of 65 years (Aging Futures Project, 1994). The New York State Department of Health calculated the prevalence of Alzheimer's disease to be 5,609 cases in the one urban and two rural counties that make up the tri-county area.

ADAC was founded in 1988 to provide clients in the tri-county area accurate diagnostic and case management services. Clients referred to ADAC are assigned a case manager, who is either an advanced practice nurse, a social worker, or a recreation therapist. One of the duties of the case manager is to assess the support and educational needs of both care receivers and caregivers. Since 1994, the assessment has included a family needs survey, to be completed by the caregiver, that includes items to evaluate the caregiver's perception of the care receiver's level of functioning. Specifically, this paper examines rural and urban families' perceptions of need in the areas of: (a) instrumental activities of daily living, (b) activities of daily living, (c) ability to keep occupied, (d) problem behaviors, (e) interest in learning new coping strategies, (f) interest in obtaining information about outside support, and (g) the participation in activities to help with coping during the past three months.

LITERATURE REVIEW

According to the 1990 census, there are 31 million Americans over the age of 65 years. Of these elders, about 8.2 million or 26% live in rural areas. It has been suggested that rurality should be viewed as a continuum of residential environments outside of cities and suburbs, whose designation is based on population number and density, as well as current and historical economic structure (Krout, 1994). However, most definitions are based on population size. The metropolitan statistical area (MSA) designation, which defines counties as metropolitan or urbanized if there is a city with a population greater than 50,000 or a total MSA population of at least 100,000, is often used (Clifford & Lilley, 1993; Krout, 1994; Weinert & Burman, 1996). The definition of rural used for this paper is based on the MSA designation. Of the three counties in the tri-county area of the Southern Tier of New York, one county contains an MSA with a population greater than 50,000 and has been designated urban. The other two counties have been designated as rural.

Even though only 26% of elderly Americans live in rural areas, the proportion of elderly people between the ages of 65 and 84 years making up the rural population is higher than in urban areas because of out-migration of young people (Krout, 1994; Clifford & Lilley, 1993). Elders in rural areas are more likely than their urban counterparts to have self-care deficits in activities of daily living (ADLs) and are less able to perform instrumental activities of daily living (IADLs), such as household chores and transportation (Coward & Cutler, 1988; Cutler & Coward, 1988; Krout, 1989). In fact, non-farm rural elders have the poorest health status (Coward, Lee & Dwyer, 1993).

Keeping the elderly in the community is financially more cost effective than institutionalizing them, but services do need to be provided to help reduce the stress felt by caregivers, thereby enabling care receivers to stay at home longer (Krout, 1994). Krout (1994) discusses the seven "A's" of providing services: availability, accessibility, awareness, acceptability, affordability, appropriateness and adequacy. Many services simply are not available or accessible in rural areas because of the cost of providing services in geographically isolated areas with low population density (Conley & Burman, 1997). Nor are the services necessarily affordable to low-income elders (Clifford & Lilley, 1993). Rural caregivers tend to be mistrustful of services provided by outsiders and uncomfortable with dealing with bureaucracy. Many services may, therefore, be unacceptable (Krout, 1994). Services provided may not be appropriate or adequate to meet the specific needs of rural elders. As an example, Lee and Gray (1992) conducted an analysis of several Senior Companion Programs in rural and urban areas and showed that the programs that had been in place the longest had the most volunteers in both rural and urban areas, indicating an ability to recruit volunteers. However, the clientele served by the programs only increased in urban areas, not in rural areas. Moreover, the number of referrals to other agencies because of inability to provide services was much greater in rural areas. This example shows the importance of meeting the criteria of the seven A's.

There is a common belief that rural elderly have a large informal network of family supports and that they have more contact with their adult children than urban elderly; however, this perception has not withstood the test of scrutiny (Krout, 1986). The primary informal helping network for elders in urban and rural areas is family, but families may be comprised of only one individual (Coward, Cutler & Mullens, 1990). While there are more formal services available to elders and their caregivers (Coward & Dwyer, 1991), rural caregivers are often unaware of the services available to them (McCabe, Sand, Yeaworth and Nieveen, 1995), and are less likely to take advantage of them if they are available (Kenney, 1993).

Caregivers of elders with dementia are more likely than caregivers of elders without dementia to use in-home services as the number and severity of ADL deficits increase and as caregiver physical strength and health decline (Gill, Hinrichsen & DiGiuseppe, 1998). Rural caregivers of elders with dementia tend to use the services available to them, if they are aware of them (McCabe et al., 1995). Dementia changes the nature of the relationship between caregivers and care receivers, which becomes task-focused, with fewer positive, loving interactions, and this markedly increases caregiver stress (Carruth, 1996).

Rural caregivers caring for elders with and without dementia spend more time performing tasks for care receivers than urban caregivers (Horwitz & Rosenthal, 1994; Dwyer & Miller, 1990b), resulting in high levels of caregiver stress and burden (Stoller & Pugliesi, 1989). Continuous care decreases personal time (Chenier, 1997) as well as the number of positive interactions between caregiver and care receiver (Carruth, 1996). Interestingly, caregivers experiencing the most burden and stress are the least likely to use respite care (Cottrell, 1996), even when the service is provided free or for a reduced fee (Bourgeois, Schulz & Burgio, 1996). Evidence is conflicted as to whether respite care leads to increased institutionalization of elders with dementia, as caregivers begin to learn what life could be like without the constant stress of caregiving (Bourgeois et al., 1996), or whether accessing respite care enables caregivers to keep care receivers in the community longer (Lawton, Brody & Saperstein, 1989). Respite care has been shown to reduce problem behaviors in care receivers with dementia by providing opportunities for care receivers to socialize and participate in activities and recreation on a regular basis (Burdz, Eaton & Bond, 1988).

METHODS

The convenience sample for this study represents non-institutionalized elders living in a three-county area in the Southern Tier of New York State, who were evaluated by the staff of the Alzheimer's Disease Assistance Center between December 1995 and May 1998. All families who were referred to the clinic during this period were surveyed for educational and support needs.

The survey was created by the Education Coordinator for use at the ADAC, and all staff were trained to use it. Test-retest and inter-rater reliability scores were acceptable at .96 or better. Those who received a diagnosis of Probable Alzheimer's disease were included in this sample. Over a period of 2 1/2 years, 76 surveys were completed by caregivers of individuals with Probable Alzheimer's disease. Data were collected by the Center's Education Coordinator as part of the family educational needs assessment, and information from each survey was used to tailor individualized educational materials and services for the family.

These data were examined and compared by splitting the sample into "rural" and "urban" components. Rural was defined as a non-metropolitan county where there is no city with a population of greater than 50,000. Two of the three counties were rural. Urban was defined as a metropolitan county, where there is a major city with a population over 50,000. These data were then analyzed using Statistical Package for Social Sciences (SPSS,1994).

Of the 76 individuals presenting with Probable Alzheimer's disease, 26% were male and 74% were female; 94.5% were white, 1.8% were African-American, and 3.6% were other races; 43.6% of the sample were married or living with a partner, 41.8% were widowed, 1.8% were divorced, and 10.9% were never married. The mean age of the individuals who were evaluated was 78.5 years. Each of the individuals with Probable Alzheimer's disease had a caregiver who responded to the needs survey.

RESULTS

All caregivers had been referred to the ADAC by another agency, or caregivers had heard about ADAC and initiated contact directly. Thirty-one caregivers were from one of two rural counties (defined by lack of a major metropolitan area), and 45 caregivers were from an urban county (defined by presence of a major metropolitan area). A total of 76 caregivers were surveyed.

Demographics of caregivers and care receivers are presented in Table 1. As expected, caregivers were predominantly female in both rural (71%) and urban (71.1%) areas. Mean age of rural caregivers was 61.1 ± 3.0 years and mean age of urban caregivers was 58.6 ± 2.4 years. Rural caregivers had been providing care for their family member with memory loss for 40.5 ± 9.1 months, while urban caregivers had been providing care for 23.7 ± 5.0 months.

Care receivers were also predominantly female in both areas of residence (67.7% rural vs. 80.0% urban). Rural care receivers were significantly older than urban care receivers (80.9 ± 1.2 vs. 77.3 ± 0.9 years, $p < 0.05$). Most rural and urban care receivers were either still married and living with their

TABLE 1. Demographics of caregivers and care receivers

Variables	Rural	Urban
Number	31	45
Caregivers		
Gender (% Female)	71.0	71.1
Age (mean ± SEM)	61.1 ± 3.0	58.6 ± 2.4
Months providing care (mean ± SEM)	40.5 ± 9.1	23.7 ± 5.0
Care Receivers		
% Female	67.7	80.0
Age (years ± SEM)	80.9 ± 1.2*	77.3 ± 0.9
Marital status		
Married	45.2	42.2
Widowed	51.6	40.0
Divorced, Separated, Other	3.4	17.7
Lives with		
Self (alone)	13.8	24.4
Spouse	44.8	42.2
Daughter	31.0	4.4
Son	-	8.9
Sibling	6.9	17.8
Other	3.4	2.2
Persons living in home (mean ± SEM)	3.91 ± 1.4	2.0 ± 0.2

*Statistically significant at $p < 0.05$

spouses (45.2% rural vs. 42.2% urban), or were widowed (51.6% rural vs. 40% urban). More rural than urban care receivers lived with a daughter (31% rural vs. 4.4% urban), while fewer rural than urban care receivers lived alone (13.8% rural vs. 24.4% urban), or with a sibling (6.9% rural vs. 17.8% urban). Finally, there tended to be more people living in the care receivers' homes in rural than in urban areas (3.9 ± 1.4 rural vs. 2.0 ± 0.2 urban).

Caregiver perception of level of functioning of care receiver was determined by asking how much assistance the care receiver required to perform ADLs, including keeping themselves occupied, and to perform IADLs, including entertaining themselves. The choices offered for level of assistance were "no assistance needed," "some assistance needed," or "always needed assistance" to complete the task. These results are presented in Table 2 as percentage of care receivers responding at each of three levels of assistance. There was no difference between rural and urban care receivers in ability to perform ADLs, and most care receivers required no assistance or only some assistance. Although there was no overall difference between rural and urban

TABLE 2. Caregiver perception of level of functioning of care receiver as measured by ability to perform ADLs and IADLs

	Rural (%)			Urban (%)		
	Assistance Needed			Assistance Needed		
	None	Some	Always	None	Some	Always
ADLs						
Activities	30.0	36.7	33.3	31.8	40.9	27.3
Eating	80.6	16.1	3.2	84.4	15.6	--
Dressing	45.2	48.4	6.5	55.6	33.3	11.1
Grooming	38.7	48.4	12.9	48.9	44.4	6.7
Bathing	45.2	25.8	29.0	42.2	42.2	15.6
Toileting	67.7	32.3	--	75.6	22.2	2.2
IADLs						
Recreation	6.7	16.7	76.7	13.3	37.8	48.9
Housework	10.7	39.3	50.0	8.9	64.4	26.7
Laundry	14.3	25.0	60.7	15.6	42.2	42.2
Shopping	6.9	17.2	75.9	6.7	37.8	55.6
Cooking	14.3	28.6	57.1	15.6	51.1	33.3
Transportation	6.7	10.0	83.3	11.1	22.2	66.7

care receivers in their ability to perform IADLs, rural care receivers were more likely to always require assistance in performing IADLs, whereas urban care receivers were more likely to need only some assistance. In addition, rural care receivers were more likely to be unable to engage in recreation without caregiver assistance (76.7% rural vs. 48.9% urban).

Percentage of caregivers interested in receiving information or education on ADLs or IADLs is presented in Table 3. The choices were "Yes–I would like educational/training materials" or "No–I don't need this information." More caregivers expressed an interest in learning new coping strategies to keep their care receivers functional in ADLs than in IADLs. Overwhelmingly, however, caregivers in both rural and urban areas were interested in learning new coping strategies to provide activities to keep care receivers busy with activities or to provide recreation for them.

Caregiver perception of certain problem behaviors exhibited by their care receivers and caregiver interest in learning new coping strategies are presented in Table 4. As with ADLs, importance of a particular behavior to the

TABLE 3. Caregiver interest in learning new coping strategies to help care receiver perform ADLs and IADLs

	Rural (%) Yes–would like information/training	Urban (%) Yes–would like information/training
ADLs		
Activities	82.1	65.1
Eating	32.0	10.0
Dressing	41.7	23.3
Grooming	40.0	23.3
Bathing	52.0	38.1
Toileting	42.3	19.0
IADLs		
Recreation	75.0	60.5
Housework	21.4	14.3
Laundry	7.1	4.9
Shopping	7.1	12.2
Cooking	17.9	11.9
Transportation	21.4	19.5

caregiver was gauged by their indication of "Yes–I would like educational/training materials" or "No–I don't need that information" on learning new coping strategies. Although there was no statistical difference between rural and urban areas for care receivers' ability to keep themselves occupied (90% rural vs. 75.6% urban), 90.3% (vs. 53.8% in urban areas) of rural caregivers expressed an interest in learning new ways to provide things to do. Rural caregivers were more likely to want to learn how to cope with restless/agitated behaviors than urban caregivers (66.7% rural vs. 43.2% urban). Urban caregivers, however, were more likely to want to learn about suspicious/accusing behavior (54.5% urban vs. 26.7% rural) and repetitive questions/actions (60% urban vs. 33.3% rural). Interestingly, care receivers in urban areas were more likely than their rural counterparts to see or hear things (51.2% urban vs. 37.9% rural), but this was of less concern to caregivers than some other problems exhibited.

Percentage of caregivers expressing an interest in obtaining information about outside support for their receiver of care is presented in Table 5. Rural caregivers were more likely than urban caregivers to be interested in having someone take their relatives out (79.3% rural vs. 45.2% urban) for recreation. There were no statistical differences between rural and urban caregivers in interest expressed in other sources of outside support.

Finally, caregivers were assessed for their participation, during the last 3

TABLE 4. Caregiver perception of percent of care receivers exhibiting problem behaviors, and caregiver interest in learning new coping strategies

	Rural (%)		Urban (%)	
BEHAVIOR	% with Behavior	Learn	% with Behavior	Learn
Inability to occupy self	90.0	90.3**	75.6	56.8
Following/clinging	56.6	51.6	63.6	34.1
Restless/agitated	83.3	66.7*	75.6	43.2
Suspicious/accusing	62.1	26.7	70.5	54.5*
Seeing/hearing things	37.9	20.0	51.2*	30.2
Repetitive questions/actions	80.6	33.3	97.8	60.0*
Inability to recognize people	66.7	23.3	86.4	40.9
Yelling/swearing	53.3	26.7	46.7	23.3
Tearful/sad/crying	60.0	40.0	60.0	38.6
Angry/aggressive	63.3	36.7	56.8	37.2
Inappropriate sexual behavior	3.3	6.7	6.7	2.3
Incontinence	50.0	30.0	42.2	25.6
Wandering	46.4	43.3	46.7	45.5
Waking caregiver at night	50.0	23.3	48.8	36.4
Getting into unsafe situations	34.5	30.0	48.9	40.9

*significant at $p < 0.05$

**significant at $p < 0.01$

months, in activities to help themselves cope better with their care receivers with dementia. Results are presented in Table 6. Rural caregivers were more likely than those in urban areas to have participated in Alzheimer's education (53.8% rural vs. 7.1% urban). There was no difference between rural and urban caregivers in their participation in other activities, nor did these activities seem to be of particular interest to caregivers, given the low level of interest in participating.

DISCUSSION

Unmet Need

Studies that have examined caregiver and care receiver needs in the past have not included questions about activities, recreation, or leisure for the

TABLE 5. Percent (%) caregivers expressing interest in accessing outside support to help with care receiver

Type of Outside Support	Rural (%)	Urban (%)
Someone to take out for recreation	79.3**	45.2
In-home sitters	64.3	65.1
Overnight respite	37.0	41.9
Regular paid help	50.0	38.6

**significant at $p < 0.01$

TABLE 6. Percent of caregivers who participated in activities to help with care of receiver during last 3 months, and percent who would like to participate

Type of activity	Rural (%)		Urban (%)	
	Participated	Would like	Participated	Would like
Alzheimer's education	53.8**	15.4	7.1	31.0
Support group	14.3	7.1	7.0	9.3
Counseling	10.3	6.9	17.8	11.1
Legal planning	20.0	10.0	22.7	15.9
Financial planning	20.7	6.9	22.7	15.9
Case management	10.3	6.9	14.3	14.3
Home modification	10.3	6.9	7.0	14.0

**significant at $p < 0.001$

individual with dementia. This is an important area to consider in the care of the individual with Alzheimer's disease because it may impact on other areas of function. Research in nursing home settings have shown that therapeutic activities can maintain or improve function in people with dementia, as well as reduce problem behaviors (Buettner, Lundegren, Lago, Farrell, & Smith, 1996; Buettner & Ferrario, 1998). If applied to individuals with dementia and their caregivers who live in urban or rural communities, overall functional status of these individuals may improve or be maintained, thus delaying premature institutionalization.

There appears to be an unmet need in the Alzheimer's family for meaningful activity and recreation for the care receiver. Activities and recreation were identified as the areas that care receivers needed the most assistance with, and the items that caregivers could not provide. Caregivers in both rural and urban settings recognized these needs as important ones and asked for education and training in these areas. Other questions in the survey also support this finding. For example, in questions about problem behaviors, caregivers in both rural and urban areas found the care receivers lack of "ability to keep busy" as a major problem. Caregivers also indicated that "restless" and "agitated" behaviors were problematic. These behaviors have been found to strongly correlate with boredom and inactivity (Cohen-Mansfield, Werner, & Marx, 1992). Finally, in the question about interest in outside services, caregivers, especially those in rural settings, were very interested in finding someone to take their family members out into the community for recreation and socialization.

This desire for help with an unmet need could be addressed by adding a therapeutic recreation specialist to the home health team or to the staff of geriatric assessment clinics. The role of recreation therapy in the home of the Alzheimer's family appears to be an important one, and one that has not been widely considered in the past.

Rural vs. Urban Differences

In planning for and providing these recreational services, it is important to realize the differing needs in rural versus urban areas. Rural care receivers were significantly older and had been cared for longer than urban care receivers. More rural than urban care receivers lived with an adult child (31% rural vs. 13.3% urban), which was contrary to expectation, as it had previously been found that rural care receivers were less likely to live with an adult child (Lee, Dwyer & Coward, 1990).

Significantly more rural than urban caregivers expressed an interest in learning new coping strategies to keep their elders busy (90.3% rural vs. 56.8% urban, $p < 0.01$), although interest in both groups was high. More rural than urban caregivers expressed an interest in learning about services that would provide someone to take their care receivers out for recreation (79.3% rural vs. 45.2% urban, $p < 0.01$). In addition, more rural care receivers were likely to always need assistance in providing recreation (76.7% vs 48.9%). Both rural and urban caregivers were equally interested in learning about at-home sitters. Respite care has been shown to decrease problem behaviors and increase care receivers' level of content (Burdz et al., 1988). In addition, use of respite care by caregivers may increase the likelihood of keeping care receivers in the community (Lawton et al., 1988), though it has not been shown to decrease caregiver burden and stress (Bourgeois et al., 1996; Lawton et al., 1988). An intervention study is required in which appropriate activities and opportunities for recreation are provided to care receivers, and which examines the effects of these interventions on caregiver burden and stress. The informal network of respite providers currently used by caregivers needs to be educated about the use of activities in the home, and a more direct measure of caregiver burden and stress needs to be developed to assess the efficacy of this intervention.

More rural than urban caregivers expressed an interest in learning how to cope with restless and agitated behaviors (66.7% rural vs. 43.2 % urban, $p < 0.05$), which can be exhibited by care receivers who do not have enough appropriate activities to keep them occupied. More urban caregivers, however, expressed an interest in learning how to cope with suspicious and accusing behaviors (26.7% rural vs. 54.5% urban, $p < 0.05$), as well as repetitive questions and actions (33.3% rural vs. 60.0% urban, $p < 0.05$). Urban caregivers had not spent as many months, nor did they spend as many hours per week in caring for their elder as rural caregivers. It is, therefore, possible that they were less tolerant of these behaviors than rural caregivers. Although it has been suggested that rural caregivers may have a greater tolerance for elders with dementia (Keefover, Rankin, Keyl, Wells, Martin, & Shaw, 1996), it is also possible that rural caregivers were no more tolerant but had been unaware of services available to them (McCabe et al., 1994).

Rural caregivers were more likely than urban caregivers to have attended an Alzheimer's Disease education program in the three months prior to completing the survey (53.8% rural vs. 7.1% urban, $p < 0.001$). This was a surprising finding and may reflect the level of education of the rural caregivers, as more highly educated caregivers do seek out information on their care receivers' conditions earlier than less educated caregivers (Conley & Burman, 1997). This warrants further investigation.

This study should be recognized as preliminary and as having several limitations. First, there was a selection bias in the study sample. The participants were all families who sought out diagnostic and case management services from the Binghamton University ADAC. This is a select group who were coming to a "center of excellence" for services after not finding adequate care elsewhere. A second limitation was that the measures of need for activities and recreation were indicated from four direct questions and two indirect questions on a longer needs assessment survey. Future work should look at these items in greater depth. Thirdly, there was a lack of gender, ethnic, and racial diversity in this sample. The majority of the sample was female and white.

CONCLUSION

The caregivers in this study believe their family members with dementia have a vital need for meaningful leisure time pursuits, but they don't know how to provide that aspect of care. Although each person with dementia is distinctive in leisure history, lifestyle, and ability to adapt to age and disease, the need for activity is clear. Caregivers in both rural and urban settings are recognizing a need and are asking for help in the area of activities and recreation for their family members with dementia. They recognize that once basic care is completed, the individual with dementia quickly becomes bored without structured activities. This information is important in planning and developing services for Alzheimer's families in the future. Further investigation is needed to examine the effects of providing these recreational services on care receivers' health and well-being, and on levels of caregiver stress and burden.

REFERENCES

Aging Futures Project of Broome County (1994). *Action for Older Persons, Inc.* (Report Series 1.0 and 1.1). Binghamton, NY: Broome County Office for Aging.

Bourgeois, M. S., Schulz R., & Burgio, L. (1996). Interventions for caregivers of patients with Alzheimer's Disease: A review and analysis of content, process, and outcomes. *International Journal of Aging and Human Development, 43,* 35-92.

Buettner, L. & Ferrario, J. (1998). Therapeutic recreation-nursing team: a therapeutic intervention for nursing home residents with dementia. *Annual in Therapeutic Recreation, 7,* 21-28.

Buettner, L., Lundegren, H., Lago, D., Farrell, P., & Smith, R. (1996). Therapeutic recreation as an intervention for persons with dementia and agitation: An efficacy study. *American Journal of Alzheimer's Disease, 11,*4-12.

Buettner, L. & Waitkavitz, J. (1998). Preventing falls in long term care: A model therapeutic recreation program. In G.L. Hitzhuzen (Ed.), *Global Therapeutic Recreation V,* (pp.101-109) Columbia: University of Missouri Press.

Burdz, M. P., Eaton, W. O., & Bond, J. B. (1988). Effect of respite care of dementia and nondementia patients and their caregivers. *Psychology and Aging, 3,* 38-42.

Carruth, A. K. (1996). Motivating factors, exchange patterns, and reciprocity among caregivers of parents with and without dementia. *Research in Nursing & Health, 19,* 409-419.

Chenier, M. C. (1997). Review and analysis of caregiver burden and nursing home placement. *Geriatric Nursing, 18,* 121-126.

Clifford, W. B., & Lilley, S. C. (1993). Rural elderly: Their demographic characteristics. In C. Bull (Ed.), *Aging in Rural America* (pp. 3-16). London: Sage Publications.

Cohen-Mansfield, J., Werner, P., & Marx, M. (1992). Observational data on time use and behavior problems in the nursing home. *Journal of Applied Gerontology, 11,* 114-117.

Conley, V. M., & Burman, M. E. (1997). Informational needs of caregivers of terminal patients in a rural state. *Home Healthcare Nurse, 15,* 808-817.

Cottrell, V. (1996). Respite use by dementia caregivers: preferences and reasons for initial use. *Journal of Gerontological Social Work, 26 (3/4),* 35-55.

Coward, R. T., & Cutler, S. J. (1988). The concept of continuum of residence: comparing activities of daily living among the elderly. *Journal of Rural Studies, 4*, 159-168.

Coward, R. T., Cutler, S. J., & Mullens, R. A. (1990). Residential differences in the composition of the helping networks of impaired elders. *Family Relations, 39*, 44-50.

Coward, R. T., & Dwyer, J. W. (1991). A longitudinal study of residential differences in the composition of the helping networks of impaired elders. *Journal of Aging Studies, 5*, 391-407.

Coward, R. T., Lee, G. R., & Dwyer, J. W. (1993). The family relations of rural elders. In C. Bull (Ed.). *Aging in Rural America* (pp. 216-231). London: Sage Publications.

Cutler, S. J., & Coward, R. T. (1988). Residence difference in the health status of elders. *Journal of Rural Health, 4*, 11-26.

Dwyer, J. W. & Miller, M. K. (1990a). Differences in characteristics of the caregiving network by area of residence: Implications for primary caregiver stress and burden. *Family Relations, 39*, 27-37.

Dwyer, J. W., & Miller, M. K. (1990b). Determinants of primary caregiver stress and burden: Area of residence and the caregiving networks of frail elders. *The Journal of Rural Health, 6*, 161-184.

Evans, D. A., (1990). Estimated prevalence of Alzheimer's disease in the United States, *The Milbank Quarterly, 68*(2), 267-289.

Gill, C. E., Hinrichsen, G. A., DiGiuseppe, R. (1998). Factors associated with formal service use by family members of patients with dementia. *Journal of Applied Gerontology, 17*, 38-52.

Keefover, R. W., Rankin, E. D., Keyl, P. M., Wells, J. C., Martin, J., & Shaw, J. (1996). Dementing illnesses in rural populations: The need for research and challenges confronting investigators. *The Journal of Rural Health, 12*, 178-187.

Kenney, G. M. (1993). Is access to home health are a problem in rural areas? *American Journal of Public Health, 83*, 412-414.

Krout, J. A. (1986). *The aged in rural America.* Westport, CT: Greenwood.

Krout, J. A. (1989). Rural versus urban differences in health dependence among the elderly population. *International Journal of Aging and Human Development, 28*, 141-156.

Krout, J. A. (1994). An overview of older rural populations and community-based services. In J. A. Krout (Ed.), *Providing community-based services to the rural elderly* (pp. 3-18). London: Sage Publications.

Lawton, M. P., Brody, E. M., & Saperstein, A. R. (1988). A controlled study of respite service for caregivers of Alzheimer's patients. *The Gerontologist, 29*, 8-16.

Lee, C. F., & Gray, L. C. (1992). Respite service to family caregivers by the senior companion program: An urban-rural comparison. *Journal of Applied Gerontology, 11*, 395-406.

Lee, G., Dwyer, J., & Coward, R. T. (1990). Residential location and proximity to children among impaired elderly parents. *Rural Sociology, 55*, 579-589.

McCabe, B. W., Sand, B. J., Yeaworth, R. C., & Nieveen, J. L. (1995). Availability and utilization of services by Alzheimer's Disease caregivers. *Journal of Gerontological Nursing, 21 (1)*, 14-22.

Stoller, E. P., & Pugliesi, K. L. (1989). Other roles of caregivers: competing responsibilities or supportive resources. *The Journal of Gerontology, 44*, S231-238.

SPSS for Windows–Standard Version (1994), SPSS, Inc.

Weinert, C., & Burman, M. E. (1996). Nursing of rural elders: Myth and reality. In E. A. Swanson & T. Tripp-Reimer (Eds.), *Advances in Gerontological Nursing, Vol. 1* (pp. 57-88). New York: Springer.

Zarit, S., Orr, N., & Zarit, J. (1985). *The hidden victims of Alzheimer's disease: Families under stress.* New York: New York University Press.

Leisure Education
with Caregiver Support Groups

Marcia Jean Carter
Ida O. Nezey
Karen Wenzel
Claire Foret

SUMMARY. The purpose of this article is to identify the needs resulting from caregiving, discuss how leisure education programs benefit
caregivers and care recipients, and provide examples of specific leisure
education strategies used in caregiver groups. Specifically, the needs of
caregivers and care recipients ameliorated through leisure experiences and
the incorporation of leisure education activities into support group processes are illustrated. Leisure education experiences conducted in support
groups offer ways to address challenges faced by caregivers while promoting improved care recipient alternatives. *[Article copies available for a fee
from The Haworth Document Delivery Service: 1-800-342-9678. E-mail address:
getinfo@haworthpressinc.com <Website: http://www.haworthpressinc.com>]*

KEYWORDS. Caregivers, care recipients, support groups, leisure education

Marcia Jean Carter, ReD, CTRS, CLP, is Associate Professor, Ashland Universi-
ty, Ashland, OH 44805.
Ida O. Nezey is Director, Older Adult Services, Lafayette General Medical Cen-
ter, Coolidge Avenue, Lafayette, LA 70501.
Karen Wenzel, MA, CTRS, CLP is Director, Rocky Mountain Multiple Sclerosis
Center, Adult Day Enrichment, 2851 West 52nd Avenue, Denver, CO 80221-1259.
Claire M. Foret, PhD, CTRS, is Professor, University of Southwestern Louisiana,
225 Cajundoe Boulevard, Lafayette, LA 70506.

[Haworth co-indexing entry note]: "Leisure Education with Caregiver Support Groups." Carter, Marcia
Jean et al. Co-published simultaneously in *Activities, Adaptation & Aging* (The Haworth Press, Inc.) Vol.
24, No. 2, 1999, pp. 67-81; and: *Caregiving–Leisure and Aging* (ed: M. Jean Keller) The Haworth Press,
Inc., 1999, pp. 67-81. Single or multiple copies of this article are available for a fee from The Haworth
Document Delivery Service [1-800-342-9678, 9:00 a.m. - 5:00 p.m. (EST). E-mail address: getinfo@
haworthpressinc.com].

INTRODUCTION

Currently, caregiving responsibilities fall primarily to those who are 45-54 years old (Cantor, 1992). Patterns of social change suggest reliance on family members to meet aging parents' needs will be a challenge faced by not only relatives but friends and neighbors in the 21st century (Thomas, 1993). Caregiving is known to be a source of considerable burden adversely affecting caregiver well-being and the ability of the caregiver to complete caregiving tasks.

Caregiving reduces available discretionary time, social activities, and the freedom to make choices and decisions (Bedini & Guinan, 1996). Caregivers tend to be unaware of the importance of leisure to their own well-being (Keller, 1992). In a recent survey, when asked what was the most difficult aspect about caregiving, caregivers ranked loss of leisure second to experiencing a sense of isolation (National Family Caregivers Association/Fortis, Inc., 1998, p. 7). While leisure experiences reduce the burden of caregiving, caregiver responsibilities and attitudes tend to create barriers to leisure opportunities that can ameliorate the social and emotional stress of formal and informal caregiving.

Caregiver support groups are effective in helping family members use more positive coping strategies, enrich family relationships, and address caregiver and care recipient needs (Dupuis & Pedlar, 1995). Education and training strategies are used in support groups to teach coping strategies. Education and training strategies like leisure education are used in support groups to teach coping strategies. "Leisure education programs may provide the key to developing mechanisms of coping" (Hagan, Green, & Starling, 1997, p. 45). Leisure education programs offer social support and resource awareness that empower enhanced well-being behaviors among caregivers. Leisure education introduced during family support groups present the importance of leisure to life satisfaction and to relieving caregiver burden.

The purpose of this article is to identify the needs resulting from caregiving, discuss how leisure education programs benefit caregivers and care recipients, and provide examples of specific leisure education strategies used in caregiver groups. Specifically, the needs of caregivers and care recipients ameliorated through leisure experiences and the incorporation of leisure education activities into support group processes will be illustrated.

CAREGIVING AND LEISURE EDUCATION

Caregivers care for others in formal and informal settings. Formal caregiving happens during visits with older adults living in assisted living centers and skilled care units while informal caregiving occurs primarily in the home among family, friends and neighbors. Caregiving creates barriers to leisure participation and necessitates changes in leisure behavior (Bedini & Guinan, 1996). Barriers to caregiver leisure are created by guilt feelings, fatigue, lack of time, and financial strain (Bedini & Guinan, 1996). Caregivers tend to experience decline in social contacts and report a lack of freedom to do as they prefer (Bedini & Guinan, 1996). Caregivers also tend to be unaware of leisure resources for themselves and the care recipient (Olsson, Rosenthal, Greninger, Pituch & Metress, 1990).

Leisure education programs are a means of facilitating behavior change and creating awareness of options and choices that mediate negative lifestyle impacts such as the stress associated with caregiving. Leisure education activities are an avenue to social support, positive coping, relationship enrichment, and the acquisition of skills, knowledge, and leisure and resource awareness necessary to enhance well-being (Dupuis & Pedlar, 1995; Hagan et al., 1997/98; Keller, 1992).

Leisure education consists of several types of programs. Those most beneficial to caregivers include leisure awareness, resource awareness, leisure skill development and social skills training. Rogers (1997) reported caregivers are not always able to integrate leisure into their lives on a routine basis. Through a leisure awareness program, caregivers become aware of how leisure develops coping skills and how care recipients benefit from family leisure experiences. Leisure awareness programs provide caregivers and their adult children with ways of relating to one another (Pillemer & Suitor, 1998). Caregivers are unaware of their own leisure preferences and activities that may be adapted to satisfy care recipients' intervention goals. Leisure resource awareness and skills development programs are conduits to acquiring activity skills and the ability to incorporate leisure into the caregiver and care recipient's daily routines.

Social skills, like asking for and receiving help and asserting oneself, are caregiver needs developed through social skills training that naturally occurs in support groups (Dupuis & Pedlar, 1995; Keller, 1992). Support groups are also a means of regaining lost social contacts and reaffirming self-esteem (Bedini & Guinan, 1996; National Family Caregivers Association, 1993). When leisure education programs are incorporated into support groups, caregivers practice making decisions and participate in activities that reconnect them to resources and networks likely to promote their well-being and create a positive perception of their caregiving tasks (Dupuis & Pedlar, 1995). When the lives of caregivers are improved, they in return can provide better care services (Hagan et al., 1997/98).

LEISURE EDUCATION IN SUPPORT GROUPS

A number of leisure education strategies have been developed and implemented during family support group sessions to ameliorate the challenges created by formal and informal caregiving. The strategies presented in this section have been designed and implemented by Certified Therapeutic Recreation Specialists (CTRSs) and social service personnel (social workers) in a hospital outreach program in a southern community and in a day treatment program in a western metropolitan area in the United States. Family support groups are comprised of caregivers whose responsibilities are caring for adults with chronic disabilities and for parents, spouses and aging adult relatives. Participation in the family support groups is voluntary. Sessions are conducted monthly with the CTRSs and social workers co-facilitating sessions. Each session lasts approximately 1-2 hours and provides the opportunity for the therapists to serve as role models for the caregivers. Format of the strategies presented was developed as a result of implementing the specific activities with caregivers and reviewing recommended outlines for individual intervention plans (Carter, VanAndel, & Robb, 1995).

The conceptual framework in which the leisure education strategies are used is the therapeutic recreation process (assessment, planning, implementation, evaluation) (Carter, VanAndel, & Robb, 1995). Therapists apply this four step process to select, organize, present and determine the effectiveness of leisure education strategies with family members. The presented strategies illustrate how the needs of caregivers and care recipients are addressed through therapeutic applications of leisure education experiences.

As noted by Stumbo (1993/94), leisure inventories are appropriately used to determine the services to be offered according to participant desires, to collect history and background information and to enhance participant experiences when intervention is not the sole intent of a program. A leisure inventory for caregivers identifies services and resources useful to caregivers, collects information on behaviors prior to and during caregiving, and is a means for group members to build social connections as they identify common lifestyle changes attributed to the assumption of caregiving roles.

The Leisure Inventory for Caregivers was designed by the Office of Older Adult Services at Lafayette General Medical Center for use in its family caregivers' support group. The inventory organizes the content according to primary caregiver needs, personal well-being, social support and resources, leisure awareness and skill development, and time management (see Figure 1). Although the Leisure Inventory for Caregivers has not been formally validated, the use of this tool in caregiver support groups has provided valuable information for facilitators and participants.

In the first section of the inventory, personal well-being, respondents report the use of behaviors that contribute to holistic health. Conversely, an absence of check marks denotes barriers to a healthy lifestyle. The use of resources and social supports is considered in the second section, network support. Accurate assessment creates an awareness of resources useful to

FIGURE 1. Leisure Inventory for Caregivers

Answer the following by putting appropriate checks in spaces provided and answering questions asked. If you have a question, please ask the facilitator.

BACKGROUND INFORMATION

1. How long have you been a caregiver? _____

2. What is care recipient's living arrangement?
   _____ lives with you (caregiver)   _____ nursing home
   _____ in apartment or own home   _____ lives at home with help
   _____ in assisted living facility   _____ lives with relative
   _____ other _____

3. What is the care recipient's relationship to you?

   _____ parent _____ sibling _____ spouse _____ other (_____)

4. What is care recipient's major diagnosis/problem?
   _____

5. What is your age?   Care recipient's age? _____
   _____ under 30   _____ 50-60
   _____ 30-40   _____ 60-70
   _____ 40-50   _____ 70 and older

6. How would you characterize your relationship with care recipient? (Check all that apply)

Before Caregiving	Now	
_____	_____	Close/loving
_____	_____	Strained
_____	_____	Burdensome
_____	_____	Demanding
_____	_____	Fulfilling
_____	_____	Adequate
_____	_____	"Roller coaster" ride

7. List your leisure activity interests.

Before Caregiving	Now
_____	_____
_____	_____
_____	_____
_____	_____
_____	_____

8. PERSONAL WELL BEING	BEFORE CAREGIVING	NOW
1) Maintain a balanced diet	_____	_____
2) Maintain adequate rest	_____	_____
3) Exercise regularly	_____	_____
4) Seek prompt medical attention for health concerns	_____	_____
5) Maintain a positive attitude	_____	_____
6) Able to express my feelings	_____	_____
7) Assertive about my needs	_____	_____
8) Take care of my spiritual needs (prayer/faith)	_____	_____
9) Use humor frequently	_____	_____
10) Practice stress management techniques (relaxation, meditation, etc.)	_____	_____

FIGURE 1 (continued)

9. NETWORK OF SUPPORT	BEFORE CAREGIVING	NOW
1) Know available community resources	_____	_____
2) Acknowledge and use personal resources (finances, transportation, personal skills, etc.)	_____	_____
3) Use resources effectively (family, community)	_____	_____
4) Receive positive reinforcement (hugs, touch)		
5) Have at least one confidant	_____	_____
6) Network with other caregivers	_____	_____
7) Spend adequate time with family and friends	_____	_____
8) Ask for help when needed	_____	_____
9) Attend support groups and education programs	_____	_____
10) Have supporters who affirm me	_____	_____

10. LEISURE AWARENESS, KNOWLEDGE, SKILLS, AND ACTIVITIES

	BEFORE CAREGIVING	NOW
1) Know and apply problem-solving skills	_____	_____
2) Able to communicate needs and desires	_____	_____
3) Participate in physical activities (exercise and sports)	_____	_____

List types of exercise and sports

_____	_____	_____
_____	_____	_____
_____	_____	_____
_____	_____	_____

4) Use leisure activities to renew self	_____	_____
5) Explore a variety of new and current leisure activities		
Hobbies	_____	_____
Cultural/educational	_____	_____
Spectator sports	_____	_____
Watching TV	_____	_____
Listening to music	_____	_____
Reading	_____	_____
Volunteerism	_____	_____
Organizations	_____	_____
6) Use community leisure resources (recreation centers, senior centers, art organizations, etc.)	_____	_____
7) Feel comfortable participating in leisure activities without care recipient	_____	_____
8) Participate in family leisure activities		
with care recipient	_____	_____
without care recipient	_____	_____
9) Reinforce socialization through leisure activities	_____	_____
10) Incorporate leisure activities with care recipient into caregiving routine	_____	_____

11. TIME MANAGEMENT

		BEFORE CAREGIVING	NOW
1)	Aware of amount of time spent on caregiving tasks (____ # of hours per day)	_____	_____
2)	Aware of amount of time spent on self (____ # of hours per day)	_____	_____
3)	Amount of time spent on leisure activities (____ # of hours per day) (____ # of hours per week)	_____ _____	_____ _____
4)	How much time spent with employment?	_____	_____
5)	How much time spent with other family obligations?	_____	_____
6)	Practice time management skills		
7)	Generally, perceive there is adequate time to accomplish all tasks	_____	_____
8)	Eliminate leisure activities because of perception of inadequate time	_____	_____
9)	Demands on time reduce opportunities for socialization	_____	_____
10)	Demands on time affect my mood and emotions	_____	_____

12. Write a personal goal and 2 outcomes based on the information obtained from the survey. (May use the back of this form.)

both the caregiver and care recipient. The leisure awareness section was organized to reflect each of the recognized components of leisure education programs: leisure resources, social skills, leisure activity skills, and leisure awareness. Caregivers identify preferences and become aware of changes in their participation patterns attributed to the presence or absence of a care recipient. Lack of time is a barrier to caregiver leisure and well-being. In the closing section of the inventory, caregivers examine the portion of time spent in obligations affected by caregiving. Use of the inventory not only assesses present functioning, but also is intended to create an awareness of caregiver needs and alternatives available to enhance the quality of the family members' interactions with care recipients.

During the initial or orientation session, the Leisure Inventory for Caregivers is completed (see Figure 2). Respondents note differences in behavior patterns by identifying whether the characteristic was present before caregiving or is currently present. The outcome of the session is the identification of individual and group goals and action plans to use in subsequent sessions. Thus, planning, the second step in the therapeutic recreation process, becomes a joint responsibility of the facilitators and group members.

Community resource directories are compiled and available from park and recreation departments, area aging agencies, outpatient and referral services and community United Way agencies. The organization of a community leisure resource finder during caregiver sessions enhances networking and

FIGURE 2. Leisure Inventory for Caregivers Activity

Description: Complete the Leisure Inventory for Caregivers and set goals for themselves.

Outcomes:

1. Complete the Leisure Inventory for Caregivers.
2. Write a leisure goal and outcome.

Materials:

Leisure Inventory for Caregivers
Pencils
Easel or Chalkboard

Before:

1. Prepare copies of the Leisure Inventory for Caregivers.
2. Set-up room with chairs/tables in a circle.

During:

1. Greet participants.
2. Ask participants to introduce themselves.
3. Facilitator discusses purpose of Leisure Inventory.
4. Participants complete the Leisure Inventory for Caregivers.
5. Discuss each category contained in the inventory.
6. On an easel or chalkboard, list the priority need in each category (for the group).
7. Select one of the needs from above and write a group goal and outcomes.
8. Brainstorm on ways group can reach the goal.
9. Develop a group action plan based on goal and brainstorming.
10. Each participant selects a need from one of the categories on his/her own inventory and develops an action plan with a goal and outcome.

Follow-Up:

1. At a subsequent meeting, plan a group activity to address one of the needs identified (see Community Resource Finder activity).
2. Discuss Leisure Inventory results individually with the group facilitator or therapeutic recreation specialist.
3. Plan individual activities to address identified needs.

Other Suggestions:

1. Partner two persons or small group and have them do an activity together. (Note: May partner based on similar needs.)
2. Plan leisure activities to meet need of caregiver while including the care recipient.
3. Have caregivers encourage other family members (especially those sharing the caregiving responsibility) to complete the Leisure Inventory for Caregivers.

cohesiveness among group members and helps family members become aware of resources and experiences for themselves and the care recipient. Participating in the Community Leisure Resource Finder activity (see Figure 3), group members work together using existing resources to build individual leisure resource directories pertinent to the interests of family members. Once developed, family members are encouraged to use the guides to plan and carry out activities with each other and their care recipient.

FIGURE 3. Community Leisure Resource Finder Activity

Description: Caregivers compile a list of community leisure resources.

Outcomes

1. Compile a list of community leisure resources.
2. Organize the resources into the following categories: hobbies, cultural/arts/educational, sports/exercise/spectator sports, entertainment, dining, senior or recreation centers, travel, outdoor, and volunteer/organizations.

Materials:

Local, regional, state telephone books, yellow pages
Daily and weekly newspapers
Brochures and newsletters from senior centers, park and recreation departments, arts/cultural/educational organizations, tourists commissions, etc.
Pencils/pens
Duplicated forms to record community resources (three-hole punched)

Before:

1. Facilitator gathers brochures, newsletters, newspapers listed in material section.
2. Request that participants bring to the meeting a 1.5 inch three ring binder with 10 divider sheets with tabs.
3. Set-up room with tables and chairs.
4. Develop, duplicate, and three-hole punch leisure resource form to include: name, address, telephone #, hours of operation, what is offered and when, description of activities or services, cost and contact person.
5. Place telephone books, brochures, newsletters, etc., on centralized table.

During:

1. Discuss the outcome of this activity.
2. Explain procedure.
3. Distribute forms and direct participants to search through resource materials, selecting and recording information on activities of interest on forms provided.
4. In binder, categorize leisure community resource forms (sports, education, outdoor, etc.) requesting that participants have at least one listing in each category.
5. Discuss findings with group.

Follow-Up:

1. Compile a group list for distribution to other caregivers.
2. At a subsequent meeting, have a group discussion on usefulness of the resource binder.
3. Caregivers make a leisure resource binder available to care recipient, where appropriate.

Other Suggestions:

1. Participants design individual community leisure resource binders.
2. Compile a list of intergenerational and family activities.

Effectiveness in implementing the strategies is influenced by the ability of the individuals to come together and function as a group. As the support group matures, a number of dynamics influence outcomes of the group experience. Organization of the leisure resource directory using existing and gathering new information embodies several tasks important to group development including active participation, goal-setting, and mutual support

(O'Morrow & Carter, 1997). Trust, cooperation, and self-awareness heighten as members jointly address caregiving issues. Family members assume increased responsibility to lead and plan activities with other group members and care recipients. As this occurs, facilitators help members realize they are regaining the social contacts, control, and opportunities for decision-making perceived to be impacted by caregiving. Therefore, as suggested by Stumbo (1993/94) in her discussion of the appropriate use of inventories with caregiver groups, implementation of specific leisure education interventions is not the sole program intent but rather serves as a means to encourage therapeutic interactions among group participants.

Group cohesion and mutual support encourage information sharing and expression of feelings helpful to the implementation of meditative and relaxation experiences. Guided imagery techniques are employed to create "stay-at-home-get-aways" intended to relieve fatigue and perceptions of time constraints. A Mini-Mental Break (see Figure 4) may also serve as a reminiscence experience enabling expression of the past that deepens relationships with care recipients. When group members feel secure and confident, they are better able to assert themselves and make their needs known. Experiences like What Nurtures Me and What I Really Need in My Life Right Now Is More . . . (see Figure 5 and 6) permit expression of feelings and encourage family members to develop positive coping strategies.

Facilitators use a number of strategies to judge the effectiveness of individual leisure education interventions and outcomes of family caregiver sessions. Formative evaluation measures are the accomplishment of outcomes identified with each strategy. Periodically, facilitators have participants revisit the Leisure Inventory for Caregivers to note self-reported changes in behaviors prior to and during caregiving as measures of their adjustment to lifestyle changes. Journaling and self-initiated tape recordings are appropriate evaluative strategies with caregiver groups (Lee & Wilhite, 1995/96; Murray, 1997). When these two approaches are used, reported outcomes become integral to group sessions. Discussions surrounding diary entries and recorded responses to experiential interactions encourage self-assessment and processing of feelings related to caregiving challenges and the illnesses and disabilities faced by caregivers and care recipients.

CONCLUSIONS

As the population ages, the face of caregiving will also change. Caregiving will increasingly become the responsibility of family, friends, and neighbors as well as a particular cohort of adult children. Coping strategies found to have positive caregiver outcomes are inherent to leisure experiences. Information seeking, problem-solving, and social support are strategies apparent

FIGURE 4. Take a Mini-Mental Break

Description: A group activity where caregivers experience a mini-mental break using guided imagery, deep breathing exercises, and music.

Outcomes:

1. Participate in a mini-mental break in a group setting.
2. Discuss how to use mini-mental breaks as a leisure activity.

Materials:

Travelogue video from local library or travel agency (suggestions: tropical setting-Hawaiian theme)
A lei for each participant
Recipes for several non-alcoholic drinks. This may be printed on a sheet of paper with art work appropriate for theme. On reverse side, print steps for mini-mental break.
Audiotape with relaxing music and ocean waves
Ingredients to prepare the drinks on the recipe card
Cups, napkins, and miniature paper umbrellas to put in drinks
Assortment of travel brochures
Audio-visual equipment
Name tags and markers
Stickers depicting theme

Before:

1. Type and duplicate drink recipes and instructions.
2. Contact someone to lead the activity if facilitator is not skilled for this activity.
3. Set-up room with soft lighting and comfortable chairs arranged in a circle. (Optional: may provide floor mats and large pillows or ask participants to bring their own for the relaxation exercises).
4. Prepare drink to be served to participants.

During:

1. Greet each participant, give lei and welcome to session.
2. Give each participant a name tag. Ask to write first name and relaxing place they would like to visit. Place stickers of their choice on the tag.
3. Each participant introduces self and is invited to comment on the destination written on the name tag.
4. Facilitator sets the mood by outlining what will be done in session. Discuss need for regular breaks from caregiving routine, benefits of such breaks, methods for taking a mini-mental break at home.
5. Tell participants about selected location in video and encourage them to imagine themselves in that setting.
6. Show video.
7. Set the mood for the breathing and relaxation exercises by dimming lights and asking participants to get in a comfortable position.
8. Conduct deep breathing exercises.
9. Facilitator leads a 5-10 minute guided imagery with music for the group using the scene set in the video.
10. Serve drinks.
11. Discuss the feelings, images and experiences of the guided imagery and breathing exercises.
12. Discuss procedures for doing this activity at home.
13. Distribute recipe sheets.
14. Each participant (on back of recipe sheets) lists the setting for his/her next mini-mental break.

FIGURE 4 (continued)

Follow-up:

1. At next meeting discuss whether participants used technique, benefits derived and frequency of breaks.
2. Compile list of participants' ideas for mini-mental breaks and distribute to group.

Other Suggestions:

1. Use mini-mental break with care recipient. (Note: May want to use slides, pictures and/or travel brochures from past shared vacations or pleasant memorable experiences.)
2. Play relaxing music and do deep breathing exercises with care recipient.

FIGURE 5. What Nurtures Me

Description: Caregivers identify some of the "little" things that replenish them, or serve as "fillers" in their lives filled with so many drainers. Caregivers are also encouraged to regularly find ways to give themselves something from their nurture list on a daily basis.

Outcomes:

1. Complete the "What Nurtures Me" worksheet.
2. Commit to select one item from the worksheet for a one week period and report the following week on the experience.

Materials:

What Nurtures Me Worksheet
Pencil
Music

Before:

1. Prepare copies of the worksheet for caregivers.
2. Set up the room with chairs/tables in a circle.
3. Prepare sound system with instrumental music.

During:

1. Greet participants/introductions.
2. Facilitator discusses the tendency of caregiver to meet other's needs, and rarely address their own needs. Utilize exemplars and invite comments from the group. Present the metaphor of "filling your own cup" before you have anything to give to others. Discuss the ramifications of depleting oneself, and burning out.
3. Facilitator discusses the purpose of the exercise. Encourage participants to identify the little things in life that bring them pleasure, and could be considered "fillers."
4. Give examples by sharing previously prepared list of fillers.
5. Turn on instrumental music.
6. Participants complete worksheet.
7. Invite participants to share, as they are comfortable, their list.
8. Let participant "borrow" good ideas from other participants, and add to their list.
9. Invite participants to use the list during the upcoming week.

Follow-up:

1. Discuss the week and the impact it had on participants at the following group meeting.

Other Suggestions:

1. Caregiver may need a schedule or form to document what they did on each day of the week, and how it made them feel.

What Nurtures Me (Worksheet)

This is a list. Share it with participants as a way of encouraging them to write their own.

When I think of nurturing myself, I think of:

Quiet
The mountains at sunset
My friend Cheri
A cup of blackberry leaf tea on a quiet morning
Making something with my hands and the satisfaction of seeing something completed.
The smell of line dried laundry
Bakeries and buying something fresh out of the oven
Wearing my favorite sweats
Listening to my favorite music
Having a fire in the fireplace
A warm sweater and socks
Roasting marshmallows
Sleeping five more minutes in the morning
A mound of pillows
Watching children at play

FIGURE 6. What I Really Need in My Life Right Now is More . . .

DESCRIPTION: Complete the "What I Really Need" worksheet and identify ways and resources to meet personal needs.

Outcomes:

1. Complete the worksheet.
2. Identify at least one need and develop a plan to successfully meet the need.

Materials:

Worksheet
Pencils

Before:

1. Prepare copies of the worksheet for caregivers
2. Set up room with chairs/tables in a circle.

During:

1. Greet participants/introductions.
2. Introduce the activity and state purpose.
3. Participants complete the worksheet.
4. Participants share, as they are comfortable, information from their worksheets.
5. Each participant selects one or two of their most significant needs, and develops an action plan to more successfully meet the need.

FIGURE 6 (continued)

6. Encourage group problem solving and sharing.
7. Encourage participants to develop time frames and objectives related to their action plan.

Follow-up:

1. At a subsequent meeting, follow-up with participants to see if they are taking steps to achieve their action plan.

What I Really Need in My Life Right Now Is More . . . Worksheet

Check the words below which fit into this sentence for you. Add any other words which are also important in your life.

vitality	self-esteem	tenderness	faith
security	recognition	caring	purpose
activity	confidence	sharing	serenity
health	motivation	music	centering
strength	knowledge/skill	laughter	focus
energy	opportunities	support	awareness
fitness	challenges	companionship	trust
relaxation	variety	romance	insight
comfort	contemplation	intimacy	structure
nutrition	accomplishments	patience	surrender
touching	control	beauty	forgiveness
sex	imagination	self-awareness	silliness
sleep	money	solitude	connections
flexibility	responsibility	spirituality	conversation
spontaneity	education	play	growth
self-control	freedom	joy	novelty

Study the qualities which you have checked. Underline the ones which you can develop by yourself. Circle the ones with which you need outside help. Check below some possible sources from whom you can receive the help you need.

family	physician	club	paid help
friends	neighbors	school	other
partner/mate	co-workers	organization	
teacher	church	employer/employee	
therapist	support group	health care provider	

in leisure education and outcomes of leisure participation. Leisure experiences are a means to overcome negative management strategies like passivity, social isolation and reduced well-being behaviors.

Leisure education experiences conducted in support groups offer ways to address challenges faced by caregivers while promoting improved care recipient alternatives. Leisure education strategies like those used in the illustrations are conduits to building networks, developing awareness of leisure needs and assets, and linking caregivers to community resources. These activities also help to eliminate real and perceived barriers like time constraints and guilt feelings. Through family support groups, leisure education strategies provide ways for caregivers to address their individual needs while promoting care recipient well-being.

REFERENCES

Bedini, L. A., & Guinan, D. M. (1996). The leisure of caregivers of older adults: Implications for CTRS's in a non-traditional setting. *Therapeutic Recreation Journal, 30* (4), 274-288.

Cantor, M. H. (1992). Families and caregiving in an aging society. *Generations, 27* (3), 67-70.

Carter, M. J., VanAndel, G. E., & Robb, G. M. (1995). *Therapeutic recreation a practical approach* (2nd Ed.). Prospect Heights, IL: Waveland Press, Inc.

Dupuis, S. L. & Pedlar, A. (1995). Family leisure programs in institutional care settings: Buffering the stress of caregiving. *Therapeutic Recreation Journal, 29* (3), 184-205.

Hagan, L. P., Green, F. P., & Starling, S. (1997/1998). Addressing stress in caregivers of older adults through leisure education. *Annual in Therapeutic Recreation, 7,* 42-51.

Keller, M. J. (1992). The role of leisure education with family caregivers. *Leisure Today, 63,* 23-25, 56.

Lee, Y., & Wilhite, B. (1995/96). Capturing the immediately recalled experience: An application of the self-initiated-tape-recording method in therapeutic recreation research. *Annual in Therapeutic Recreation, 6,* 64-72.

Murray, S. B. (1997). The benefits of journaling. *Parks & Recreation, 32* (5), 68-75.

National Family Caregivers Association/Fortis Inc. (1998). *A National Family Caregivers Association/Fortis Report: Family caregiving demands recognition: Caregiving across the life cycle.* Deerfield Beach, FL: Adult Care, Inc.

National Family Caregivers Association. (Summer, 1993). A support group guide: Questions, answers, and explanations. *Take Care.* Summer, 1993, 5-7.

Olsson, R. H., Rosenthal, S. G., Greninger, L. O., Pituch, M. J. & Metress, E. S. (1990). Therapeutic recreation and family therapy: A needs analysis of wives of stroke patients. *Annual in Therapeutic Recreation, 1,* 15-20.

O'Morrow, G. S., & Carter, M. J. (1997). *Effective management in therapeutic recreation service.* State College, PA: Venture Publishing Company, Inc.

Pillemer, K. & Suitor, J. J. (1998). Baby boom families: Relations with aging parents. *Generations, XXII* (1), 65-69.

Rogers, N. B. (1997). Centrality of the caregiving role and integration of leisure in everyday life: A naturalistic study of older wife caregivers. *Therapeutic Recreation Journal, 31* (4), 230-243.

Stumbo, N. J. (1993/94). The use of activity interest inventories in therapeutic recreation assessment. *Annual in Therapeutic Recreation, 4,* 11-20.

Thomas, J. L. (1993). Concerns regarding adult children's assistance: A comparison of young-old and old-old parents. *Journal of Gerontology, 48,* (6), 315-322.

Innovative Family and Technological Interventions for Encouraging Leisure Activities in Caregivers of Persons with Alzheimer's Disease

Soledad Argüelles
Adriana von Simson

SUMMARY. This article explores the effect that a Family-Based Structural Multisystems In-Home Interventions (FSMII) with a Computer Telephone Integration System (CTIS) has on caregivers of persons with Alzheimer's disease in their ability to engage in leisure activities. It describes, from the caregivers' point of view, how their engagement in leisure activities has been negatively affected. Drawing from these personal experiences, this document illustrates the uniqueness of FSMII with CTIS in working through the barriers that caregivers encounter in the process of accessing/engaging in leisure activities. *[Article copies available for a fee from The Haworth Document Delivery Service: 1-800-342-9678. E-mail address: getinfo@haworthpressinc.com <Website: http://www.haworthpressinc.com>]*

Soledad Argüelles, PhD, is Research Assistant Professor, and Adriana von Simson, MSW, is Senior Research Associate, Center on Adult Development and Aging, Department of Psychiatry and Behavioral Sciences, University of Miami Medical School, 1425 NW 10th Avenue, Sieron Building, 2nd Floor, Miami, FL 33136.

This research was upported by the National Institute on Aging and National Institute of Nursing Research grant U01-AG13297-01.

[Haworth co-indexing entry note]: "Innovative Family and Technological Interventions for Encouraging Leisure Activities in Caregivers of Persons with Alzheimer's Disease." Argüelles, Soledad, and Adriana von Simson. Co-published simultaneously in *Activities, Adaptation & Aging* (The Haworth Press, Inc.) Vol. 24, No. 2, 1999, pp. 83-97; and: *Caregiving–Leisure and Aging* (ed: M. Jean Keller) The Haworth Press, Inc., 1999, pp. 83-97. Single or multiple copies of this article are available for a fee from The Haworth Document Delivery Service [1-800-342-9678, 9:00 a.m. - 5:00 p.m. (EST). E-mail address: getinfo@haworthpressinc.com].

83

KEYWORDS. Alzheimer's disease, caregiving, leisure, barriers, family intervention, technological intervention

Leisure means being able to take a shower in peace and quiet

–Caregiver of a person with Alzheimer's disease

INTRODUCTION AND PURPOSE

Professionals working with the elderly face two challenging tasks: (1) overcoming the barriers that prevent the elderly from engaging in leisure activities; and (2) motivating them to participate in these activities. This manuscript will summarize alternative uses of the term "leisure," and it will review prior work done in the field of leisure enhancement and promotion. Moreover, it will provide factual information regarding the importance that engaging in leisure activities has for caregivers of Alzheimer's persons. This manuscript will conclude describing the use of innovative family and technological interventions for encouraging leisure activities in this specific cohort of older caregivers. The personal accounts of caregivers will illustrate the uniqueness of the aforementioned interventions in working through the barriers that caregivers encounter in their endeavors of accessing/engaging in leisure activities.

REVIEW OF THE DEFINITION OF THE TERM "LEISURE"

Often, leisure is defined as freedom. Therefore, it is important to identify, as part of its definition, the experience of freedom of choice as well as the internal pleasure enmeshed in the meaning of the word (Kelly, 1982; Iso-Ahola, 1982; Waldman, 1993; Hughes & Keller, 1992). Iso-Ahola (1982) defines leisure as "the experience of freedom and intrinsic satisfaction rather than time allocated to specific activities" (p. 92). Another important descriptor of leisure has been its potential to provide both meaning and a sense of identity to the lives of individuals (Bundy & Cannella, 1994; Myers, 1984). In fact, Ames and Youatt (1994) support Kelly (1982) when they recommend that in order for individuals to maintain their engagement in leisure activities, these "activities must have value and meaning to the participants" (p. 763). Although molded by the above definitions, this document will focus on the special meaning of leisure in the lives of caregivers of persons with Alzheimer's disease.

FACTS ABOUT ALZHEIMER'S DISEASE AND CAREGIVING

Alzheimer's disease is the most frequent cause of irreversible dementia (loss or impairment of mental powers) in adults (Mace & Rabins, 1991). The U.S. Bureau of the Census reports that the elderly population 65 and older reached the 33.2 million mark, and that by the year 2050, 80 million Americans will be 65 or older (May, 1995). With the *graying of America* (the elderly population is both increasing and becoming older), the number of individuals who suffer from a dementing process such as Alzheimer's is also increasing. In fact, the Alzheimer's Association (1998) has projected that by the year 2040, 14 million elderly will suffer from Alzheimer's disease. Moreover, according to Guterman and Eisdorfer (1989) dementia affects 15% of the elderly in the United States.

Due to the cognitive/physical/mental impairments that individuals with dementia exhibit, they require a caregiver who provides services ranging from supervision to performance of the patients' activities of daily living (ADLs) such as bathing or feeding. Thus, caring for a family member who suffers from Alzheimer's disease is very demanding, and often the caregiver resources such as time and money are compromised. It is estimated that the annual unpaid care provided by relatives of a person with Alzheimer's disease who resides at home would be valued at over $34,000 per patient (Max, Webber, & Fox, 1995). In spite of the demands, Haley (1997) reports that family members still provide 80% of the care of Alzheimer's patients in the community.

Whether it is Alzheimer's disease or another type of dementia, caregivers must deal with the vast array of symptoms stemming from the disorder. In addition to the cognitive impairments, especially memory loss, caregivers are also faced with symptoms which are found to be related to the diagnosis of Alzheimer's disease, for example, depression, insomnia, incontinence, delusions, illusions, hallucinations, catastrophic verbal, emotional, or physical outbursts, sexual disorders, and weight loss (McKhann et al., 1984). Supplementary to coping with their grief as well as with the cognitive, behavioral, and physical difficulties of the individuals with Alzheimer's disease, caregivers report spending an average of about 60 hours per week on caregiving responsibilities (Haley et al., 1995; Max, Webber, & Fox, 1995).

Given the arduous work in which caregivers engage, both their mental and physical health are negatively affected (Haley et al., 1995; Schulz, O'Brien, Bookwala, & Fleissner, 1995; Cohen & Eisdorfer, 1988; Haley et al., 1987; Moritz, Kasl, & Berkman, 1989; Pruchno & Potashnik, 1989). For example, 30 to 50% of caregivers of persons with Alzheimer's suffer from a clinical depressive disorder (Haley et al, 1987; Haley et al., 1995) and overall they are more likely to be diagnosed with hypertension and diabetes (Levine & Lawlor, 1991).

BENEFITS OF LEISURE ENGAGEMENT

The strain of caregiver obligations makes participating in leisure activities not a luxury but a necessity for caregivers. Wheaton (1985) found that active participation in social activities is a "deterrent" against burden. Cohen and Eisdorfer (1993) also recommend that to alleviate the depression that might be precipitated by caregiving, caregivers must find activities that give them pleasure. Thompson, Futterman, Gallagher-Thompson, Rose, and Lovett (1993) also describe the importance of leisure as a "distraction" from the hardships of caring. In addition, they found that caregivers' engagement and socialization with relatives and friends (as a form of leisure) were responsible for caregivers' diminishing burden, while paucity of these leisure activities was positively correlated with feelings of being overwhelmed. Finally, Searle and Mahon (1991) report that leisure experiences enhance elderly individuals' psychological well-being.

However, several studies have shown that the responsibility of providing care for impaired older adults caregivers can have negative effects on caregivers' level of leisure involvement (Horowitz, 1985; Thompson et al., 1993; Rose & Del Maestro, 1990; Hughes & Keller, 1992). The need for professional interventions in assisting caregivers to engage in leisure activities has also been argued by Hughes and Keller (1992). They suggest that counseling and processing feelings (individually or in groups) may be critical in order to utilize respite care and engage in leisure involvement.

LEISURE MODELS

Hughes and Keller (1992) and Bundy and Cannella (1994) describe two comprehensive models of addressing leisure participation in caregivers. Hughes and Keller encourage a leisure education model based on leisure awareness, leisure activity skills, leisure resources, and social skills. Bundy and Cannella's model addresses the importance of the individual's identity enhancement by leisure, and it outlines four important components of leisure: control over the selected activities, motivation to participate in leisure tasks, disengagement from life's daily limitations, and the individual's ability to be absorbed in the leisure activity. Bundy and Cannella's model emphasizes that these four elements are crucial for an experience to be considered leisure.

Overcoming the barriers that can prevent older people in general from engaging in leisure activities as well as motivating them to participate in these activities are two areas which have been identified as important. Munson and Munson (1986) employed a form of leisure counseling that is based on Bandura's social learning theory (Bandura, 1977). It focuses on the psychological, physical, and social barriers encountered when attempting to benefit from leisure activities. Leisure counseling explores seven areas of an individual's life that may impact his/her leisure activities: health, emotions, learning, personal relationships, interests, need to know, and guidance of behavior. Losier, Bourque, and Vallerand (1992) conclude that perceptions of leisure opportunities and perceptions of leisure constraints are significant determinants of leisure motivation, and that leisure satisfaction is a good predictor of leisure participation.

DESCRIPTION OF THE REACH PROJECT

The Center on Adult Development and Aging at the University of Miami is currently investigating these issues revolving around caregiving as part of a state of the art project. The REACH project (Resources for Enhancing Alzheimer's Caregiver Health) is a multi-site project sponsored by the National Institute on Aging and the National Institute of Nursing Research. This research project involves families that have a relative living at home who suffers from Alzheimer's disease. It includes families from two ethnic groups: Euro-American and Cuban-American. Nonetheless, ethnic differences are beyond the scope of this manuscript. REACH examines the ability of three different therapeutic treatments to improve the overall functioning and adaptation of families caring for a person with dementia. The main goals of REACH are to assist both primary and secondary caregivers to: (1) reduce their objective and subjective burden, (2) reduce their distress, (3) improve their perceived social support, and (4) improve their satisfaction. Though the REACH project was not designed to enhance leisure, the topic has become an important component of the project. After working with the REACH caregivers for 2.5 years, we have experienced that on numerous occasions the aforementioned goals are achieved if caregivers engage in leisure activities. Therefore, we have addressed the need to surpass the barriers which caregivers may encounter when accessing/engaging in leisure activities.

At the present time 140 caregivers (105 female and 35 male; 65 Euro-American and 75 Cuban-American) from the Greater Miami and vicinity areas, and their families are enrolled in the REACH project. The number of participants will increase since the project will be recruiting families for 3 more months. Over 67% of these caregivers are providing care to their spouses, while approximately 27% of the caregivers are the children of the person with Alzheimer's disease. The mean age of the REACH caregivers is 70 years; this is the reason why the literature on leisure engagement in both caregivers and in the elderly in general is important. Although each family is enrolled in the project for 18 months, the intervention portions, whose descriptions follow, take place during the first 12 months. Caregivers and their families participate in assessment interviews once every 6 months, for a total of 4 assessments (baseline, 6-month, 12-month, and 18-month). Because of the nature of the project, most measures, except a Social Activities form, are not directly connected with leisure engagement. Assessment data also include measures on the caregivers' depression, anxiety, perceived burden, physical health, and support system among others, as well as demographic information on both caregivers and the persons with Alzheimer's disease. Although the REACH project is composed of three therapeutic treatments, only two will be discussed since they are the most intensive and relevant to the scope of this document: A Family-Based Structural Multisystems In-Home Intervention (FSMII) and a Computer Telephone Integration System (CTIS).

DESCRIPTION OF THE FSMII

The origin of FSMII stems from the experiences of Szapocznik and colleagues in working with depressed elderly Cuban-born individuals (Szapocznik, Santisteban, Hervis, Spencer, & Kurtines, 1981). The focus of this intervention was altering the relationships between the elderly individual and his/her environment. The challenge for FSMII is to enhance the repertoire of accessible family, community, and formal support resources available to the caregiver, and to facilitate the capacity of the caregiver and family to collaborate in the caregiving effort. The FSMII therapist meets with the caregiver, family members, and anyone significant in the caregiving system, and facilitates their interactions, which in turn, enhances the caregiving system. These meetings are usually held at the caregivers' home, therefore providing the therapists with first hand experience of how caregivers deal with the daily hardships of caretaking. The therapist usually meets with the families for approximately one hour sessions. During the first four months the meetings are held weekly, during the next two months they are held bi-weekly, and for the last six months of FSMII the therapist works with the caregivers and their families once a month.

Caregivers' Definition of the Term "Leisure"

Our work with caregivers of persons with Alzheimer's has taught us that before starting a discussion about leisure involvement, the therapists must learn about the caregiver's definition of and resistance to leisure. The therapist, caregiver, and family members form a working alliance or relationship which is especially important when the therapist facilitates specific interactions that can potentially yield changes in the caregiving system, such as leisure engagement, for instance. Therapists encounter some caregivers who are reluctant to even discuss leisure engagement, so these therapists might then refer to "leisure" as caregivers' need for "respite." These caregivers are usually more accepting of the concept of having a short-term relief or an opportunity for time-out than of having "fun."

Barriers That Could Hinder Caregivers to Engage in Leisure Activities

FSMII therapists were asked to produce examples of the constraints that caregivers of Alzheimer's persons face when engaging in leisure activities. They reported the following episodes:

- A 72-year-old caregiver providing care for her 79-year-old severely demented husband described: "I used to be a very active person all my life. My hobby, which was also my work, was decorating straw hats and handbags (shows pictures of her creative work to her therapist). I used to spend my time designing little flowers to embroider in the hats. You can see from the pictures that this work needs a lot of concentration, is very delicate. And, of course, it takes a lot of time! Which at the present time would be impossible; my husband needs me."
- A 67-year-old caregiver who is responsible for her 75-year-old mildly demented sister replied: "I used to go out for a walk every morning with my husband, just an hour of morning exercise. Ever since my sister began to exhibit the signs of Alzheimer's disease, we cannot walk. I do not really engage anymore in leisure activities as I used to. I also stopped going downstairs to the lobby to talk with my neighbors. I used to enjoy meeting and socializing with people, but these have become a hassle. Also, my sister makes odd remarks and people do not understand her. Honestly, I feel very uncomfortable. There is not real time off when you are a caregiver."
- An 81-year-old caregiver succinctly summarized in three words why she can no longer engage in leisure activities: "Energy, Time, and Money."
- A 76-year-old female caregiver of her moderately demented husband stated: "I feel so tired . . . I have no energy left to have fun."

Even though engaging in leisure activities can reduce the level of stress that caregivers are exposed to while taking care of their family members, caregivers feel guilty about "having fun" while their demented family member is being taken care of by someone else (Brody, 1985; Pratt, Schmall, & Wright, 1987). To avoid these feelings of guilt, some caregivers may choose not to engage in leisure activities at all. For example, a 62-year-old caregiver related to her therapist the following emotional dilemma. She went on a cruise with a group of friends and had such a wonderful time that she wanted to stay away from her mother and never return home to her caregiving role. She reported to her therapist: "Going on the trip affected me so much that it was harder on me than as if I had never gone. When I go out and have fun it's like living in a different world; outside is the world of the living, when I come home everything turns into illness. I have difficulty managing both worlds. I sometimes feel guilty."

Some caregivers feel a sense of reciprocity or moral obligation to pay back what was given to them by the demented person (Pratt, Schmall, & Wright, 1987). This sense of reciprocity might be one of the underlying reasons for some caregivers feeling guilty delegating to others the task of caring for their family members. Some caregivers feel that "repayment" does not leave room for having leisure. For example, a 52-year-old caregiver reports that she will do anything for her 80-year-old severely demented mother because her mother took care of her when she was a child and when she got a divorce. A 70-year-old gentleman who also feels the duty to care for his 64-year-old moderately demented wife reports: "I need to be near my wife; this is the time when she needs me the most; if I were the sick one, she would take care of me. I cannot walk away from her now. My job is here with my wife now. My life has changed."

Implementation of FSMII

FSMII does not directly follow a leisure-enhancement protocol. It uses techniques which facilitate family support and behaviors, including leisure involvement, which will ultimately help caregivers release their distress and the overall emotional and physical burden imposed on them by their caregiving role. On some instances, REACH therapists serve as educators and inform caregivers not only about the risk of their burdensome role, but about opportunities for leisure. Although it is preferred that family members cooperate with ideas, REACH therapists could inform caregivers about retirement centers, special interest clubs, continuing education courses for retired professionals, a book fair, or even an Alzheimer's support group. An intrinsic part of re-defining leisure is to teach family members and friends to recognize and advise the caregivers about their need to engage in activities like the above mentioned which will put some distance between them and the person with Alzheimer's disease.

In order to overcome the caregivers' unwillingness to accept respite, several techniques have proven to be useful. Capitalizing on giving other family members or friends the honor or opportunity to help the patient appears to be beneficial. The only way that a 52-year-old caregiver allowed her brother to provide respite care was by maximizing on her need to allow her brother, whom she loves very much, to do as she had been doing for their mother. It was further discussed that if the patient were to pass away tomorrow, she would have been fulfilled after a job well-done, but the same could not be said about her brother. She was depriving her brother of the opportunity for a meaningful experience. Her brother needed the caregiver to facilitate the opportunity to care for their mother, and thus help him feel good about it. In summary, by the brother supervising the mother, the caregiver could take a nap and visit family members, which translate into leisure activities.

A similar problem which the REACH therapists face while working with the caregivers is the caregivers' perception that no one cares, nor visits, nor is willing to assist them in providing respite care. Although these may be true in some cases, we have found that it is actually a distorted perception. By reframing the behaviors of family members and friends, and facilitating their interactions, it has been our experience that many people are more than willing to help. We have found, though, that caregivers may need to be structured and constant in their requests. Also, individuals around the caregiver may have already given up on asking to offer their assistance, or inviting the caregiver to go here or there, because they have been rejected before. In order to change these interactions the therapist capitalizes on a dialogue which might include expressing how angry, hurt or frustrated these individuals might be at the caregiver. Also, reframing the rejecting behavior as an attempt to protect the relatives from a burdensome task, and not as a negative attitude has proven to be helpful. Moreover, the therapists facilitate interactions carrying the message that helping might be burdensome to family members, but that they are truthfully offering. Overall, the positive intentions of both parties (relatives and caregivers) are highlighted as a sign of love and care.

In addition to being more accepting of the concept "respite," we have found that caregivers are more willing to engage in leisure activities if it meets another important need such as following a physician's "prescription" due to a medical condition. Hughes and Keller (1992) also recommend the "endorsement of health care professionals" (p. 126) to minimize caregivers resistance to engage in leisure activities. Regarding this matter, a 76-year-old caregiver stated: "I swim three times a week because my doctor recommended swimming for my arthritis. I have no choice but to leave my wife three hours a week." When asked whether he enjoyed this activity, the caregiver responded that it meant a lot to him because he met other people at the pool with whom he talks and spends a pleasant time away from the daily caregiving routine.

A dilemma which caregivers face is that if they wish to continue being the ones providing care for the patients, they need to not care for the patients on certain occasions. In this case the FSMII therapists highlight the caregiver's need to engage in leisure activities for the sake of the patient, not the caregiver's. Therapists facilitate interactions which will reinforce the caregiver's wonderful job, and that since no one will be able to do such a good job, the caregiver needs to do anything it takes, including accepting offers to take a break, to continue providing care to the demented patient (Pearlin, Mullan, Semple, & Skaff, 1990; Zarit & Zarit, 1982). If the caregiver becomes impaired due to overwhelming stress or burden, someone else (perhaps nursing home staff) will need to take over his/her job, and this secondary caregiver might not do the job as "perfect" as the primary caregiver. Overall, if caregivers do not take advantage of respite care early on their physical/mental well-being may be compromised, and in return, this may hinder their caregiving abilities.

A need which may prompt caregivers to engage in leisure activities is the need to help others who are perceived as helpless and less fortunate. Perhaps this is an example of what Ames and Youatt (1994) meant when they described that leisure activities must have value and meaning. A 52-year-old caregiver, although highly criticized by her relatives who feel she "has enough" with her demented mother, only leaves her house to help others. This caregiver feels useful and able to get away from her daily routine either by driving a newly arrived immigrant to the Immigration and Naturalization Office, or by visiting a relative at the hospital. It may be surprising to some that, to a burdened caregiver, the definition of leisure takes such unique meaning. It is important to know that helping others can provide moments of leisure to an otherwise burdened caregiver. This pattern of behaviors was not surprising given the life history of this lady. Even prior to becoming a caregiver she would have probably chosen to carry out altruistic behaviors over going to a social function, for example. Nonetheless, her family members were exhorted to encourage her engagement in the leisure activities she chose, even if they did not consider them as such. Again, the definition of leisure from early on in treatment is very important.

DESCRIPTION AND IMPLEMENTATION OF THE CTIS

The second major component of the REACH intervention is the Computer-Telephone Integration System (CTIS) and it is intended to augment the efficacy of FSMII. Sullivan and Searle (1994) discussed " . . . that if successful aging can be promoted, then helping professionals must employ appropriate technology to assist this process" (p. 61). Czaja, Guerrier, and Nair (1993) also found that the use of technology was positive in the elderly. They found that one of the primary reasons for the elderly to use a personal computer which had been installed in their homes was the ability to meet and communicate with people they had not previously met.

The CTIS system involves the usage of screen phones which have both text and voice. The screen phones are installed at the caregiver's home, and a trained therapist explains the mechanism. The phone installation/training is conducted according to a set protocol over three family meetings. The training not only entails the installation of the screen phone, but also deliverance of written instructions, demonstration of how to use the screen phone, the therapist completing an observation checklist of the caregivers using the phone, and caregivers answering a short questionnaire about their understanding of the system. Therapists can provide additional training if caregivers were to need it. We have experienced, though, that most caregivers are able to use the phone with no difficulties.

In addition to having the same features as a regular phone, the screen phone, which is linked to a computer system, allows caregivers to send and receive messages, leave and receive reminders, access databases with information regarding Alzheimer's disease and related services, and conference with up to six individuals at the same time. This latter feature is used to conduct caregivers' on-the-phone discussion (support) groups, therapy sessions which enhance family members' interactions, as well as spontaneous conference calls with friends and family members who might be unable to be physically present at the caregiver's home. One advantage of the screen phone over a computer linked to electronic mail is that the phone entails a more personal component. Caregivers can hear and talk to family members, friends, and other caregivers. Also, it is more accessible financially to provide caregivers with screen phones than with computers. A third advantage of the screen phone is that it is smaller than a computer. Finally, the skills required to use a screen phone are less complex than those required to use a computer.

The CTIS system serves several important roles in leisure engagement. Perhaps the greatest practical barriers which the system overcomes is the lack of transportation, inaccessible meeting places, or scheduling conflicts which many caregivers experience (Wright, Lund, Pett, & Caserta, 1987). The system also allows caregivers to provide the necessary supervision to the patient at the same time that they use the special phone.

This special phone not only enhances the communication among family members and friends which will then result in the enhancement of leisure participation by the caregivers, but it also provides a leisure experience itself. Kelly's (1983) findings argue that in adults who reside with other family members, family interaction itself is the dominant form of leisure, supporting the idea of caregivers enjoying themselves by just communicating with their relatives. This appears to be true even if the communication is via phone. We have found that even the phone installation at the home provides moments of leisure to the caregivers. Caregivers enjoy learning how to operate what they perceive to be a technological apparatus, and this knowledge makes them feel important. Some of the caregivers even teach their family members how to operate the special phone, thus providing value and meaning to the experience.

Another component of the CTIS which contributes to the engagement of caregivers in leisure activities is participation in the CTIS discussion group. The discussion group has been a great validation to the caregivers about their need for respite. Some group members are great lobbyists of many clinical issues related to caregiving, but especially about "taking a break." Hughes and Keller (1992) discussed that one of the ways in which a family support group could be advantageous is by assisting " . . . caregivers in identifying personal, family and community resources that could enable them to engage in leisure" (p. 121). It appears that caregivers will be more willing to engage in a leisure activity, such as the support group, if they perceive it as helpful to the person with Alzheimer's disease.

It has been our experience that the socialization component is very helpful to caregivers. A 75-year-old caregiver of her moderately demented husband reports with great enthusiasm that although she knows that no one will see her, she puts lipstick on and fixes her hair in order to participate in the discussion group. Caregivers usually exchange phone numbers so they can call each other outside of the group time. Some of them have arranged to meet for lunch or for other caregiving activities. The group experience has been so positive that through the information shared by other members, some of the caregivers have begun to attend community support groups or engage in other types of social or leisure-related activities.

CONCLUSIONS, IMPLICATIONS, AND FUTURE DIRECTIONS

Although the need of caregivers of persons with Alzheimer's to have some moments of leisure is well known, their participation in leisure activities is not always a reality. Caregivers' accounts of their caretaking experiences demonstrate that due to both internal and external barriers, caregivers are restricted in their ability for respite. It appears that the REACH family and technological interventions offer an alternative to assist the older caregivers overcome some of these barriers. La Rue (1993) points out that one of the challenges to mental health professionals for the aging population is the provision of education, support, and preventive interventions to strengthen older people and their families, and this is what has been envisioned when helping caregivers participate in leisure activities.

An implication of what has been illustrated in this document is that even when the REACH project was not meant to specifically target the enhancement of leisure activities, leisure has become a crucial topic of the REACH interventions. Other important implications stemming from this document are: (1) the need to clarify the meaning of leisure; (2) the ability of older caregivers to use a technological device; and (3) the importance of the support of other family members in the caregivers' endeavor to engage in leisure activities. The REACH project is currently taking place, so empirical results are not available yet. It will be interesting to see if the above descriptions are powerful enough to yield significant statistical results. It might be important to assess whether caregivers involved in FSMII or CTIS experience an increase of satisfaction in the amount of time they were able to spend in social activities (data from the Social Activities form), and whether this correlates with caregivers' depression or anxiety indexes.

It appears that future projects should address leisure involvement in the caregivers of persons with Alzheimer's disease more empirically. The impact of ethnicity on the engagement of caregivers in leisure activities appears to be the next logical step to follow for future analysis. An in depth investigation of the differences, if any, between caregivers' external barriers (e.g., transportation, time) to leisure, and caregivers' internal barriers (e.g., guilt, compensation) might also be of interest. The interventions to address the different barriers might prove to be very different. Finally, future projects might also like to address the use of the FSMII and CTIS to enhance leisure in elderly caregivers of persons with impairments such as developmental disabilities.

REFERENCES

Alzheimer's Association. (1998). *Alzheimer's Disease Resource Directory: 1998-99.* (7th ed.). Miami, FL: Author.

Ames, B. D., & Youatt, J. P. (1994). Intergenerational education and service programming: a model for selection and evaluation of activities. *Educational Gerontology, 20,* 755-764.

Bandura, A. (1977). *Social learning theory.* Englewood Cliffs, NJ: Prentice-Hall.

Brody, E. (1985). Parent care as a normative family stress. *The Gerontologist, 25,* 19-29.

Bundy, A., & Cannella, J. M. (1994). Leisure. In B. R. Bonder & M. B. Wagner (Eds.), *Functional performance in older adults* (pp. 165-180). Philadelphia: F. A. Davis Company.

Bureau of the Census. (1995, May). *Sixty-five plus in the United States* (Statistical Brief No. 95-8). Washington, DC: U. S. Department of Commerce. Economics and Statistical Administration.

Cohen, D., & Eisdorfer, C. (1988). Depression in family members caring for a relative with Alzheimer's Disease. *Journal of the American Geriatric Society, 36,* 885-889.

Cohen, D., & Eisdorfer, C. (1993). *Seven steps to effective parent care.* New York: G.P. Putnam's Sons.

Czaja, S. J., Guerrier, J., Nair, S. N., Landauer, T. K. (1993). Computer communication as an aid to independence for older adults. *Behavior and information Technology, 12,* 197-207.

Guterman, A., & Eisdorfer, C. (1989). Early diagnosis of dementias. In M. Bergener & B. Reisberg (Eds.), *Diagnosis and treatment of senile dementia* (pp. 177-192). Holland: Springer-Verlag Berlin-Heidelberg.

Haley, W. E. (1997). The family caregiver's role in Alzheimer's disease. *Neurology*, *48*, S25-S29.

Haley, W. E., Levine, E. G., Brown, S. L., Berry, J. W., & Hughes, G. H. (1987). Psychological, social and health. Consequences of caring for a relative with senile dementia. *Journal of the American Geriatric Society, 35*, 405-411.

Haley, W. E., West, C. A. C., Wadley, V. G., Ford, G. R., White, F. Y., Barrett, J. J., Harrell, L. E., & Roth, D. L. (1995). Psychological, social, and health impact of caregiving: a comparison of black and white dementia family caregivers and noncaregivers. *Psychology and Aging, 10*, 540-552.

Hogden, K. M. (1985). Leisure/recreation needs of hospitalized elderly: a task force report. *Activities, Adaptation & Aging, 7*, 53-65.

Horowitz, A. (1985). Family caregiving to the frail elderly. *Annual Review of Gerontology and Geriatrics, 5*, 194-246.

Hughes, S. & Keller, M. J. (1992). Leisure education: a coping strategy for family caregivers. *Journal of Gerontological Social Work, 19*, 115-128.

Iso-Ahola, S. E. (1980). *Social psychological perspectives on leisure and recreation*. Springfield, IL: Charles C. Thomas.

Kelly, J. R. (1982). *Leisure*. Englewood Cliffs, NJ: Prentice-Hall.

Kelly, J. R. (1983). *Leisure identities and interactions*. London: Allen & Unwin.

La Rue, A. (1993). *Aging and neuropsychological assessment*. New York: Plenum Press.

Levine, J., & Lawlor, B. A. (1991). Family counseling and legal issues in Alzheimer's disease. *The Psychiatric Clinics of North America, 14*, 385-396.

Losier, G. F., Bourque, P. E., & Vallerand, R. J. (1992). A motivational model of leisure participation in the elderly. *The Journal of Psychology, 127*, 153-170.

Mace, N. L., & Rabins, P.V. (1991). *The 36-hour day* (revised edition). New York: The Johns Hopkins University Press.

Max, W., Webber, P., & Fox, P. (1995). Alzheimer's disease: The unpaid burden of caring. *Journal of Aging Health, 7*, 179-199.

McKhann, G., Drachman, D., Folstein, M., Katzman, R., Price, D., & Stadlan, E. M. (1984). Clinical diagnosis of Alzheimer's disease: Report of the NINCDS-ADRDA work group under the auspices of Department of Health and Human Services Task Force on Alzheimer's disease. *Neurology, 34*, 939-944.

Moritz, D. J., Kasl, S. V., & Berkman, L. F. (1989). The health impact of living with a cognitively impaired elderly spouse: depressive symptoms and social functioning. *Journal of Gerontology: Social Sciences, 44*, S17-S27.

Myers, J. E. (1984). Leisure counseling for older people. In E. T. Dowd (Ed.), *Leisure counseling: Concepts and applications*, (pp. 157-177). Springfield, IL: Thomas.

Munson, W. W., & Munson, D. G. (1986). Multimodal leisure counseling with older people. *Activities, Adaptation & Aging, 9*, 1-15.

Pearlin, L. I., Mullan, J. T., Semple, S. J., & Skaff, M. M. (1990). Caregiving and the stress process: An overview of concepts and their measures. *The Gerontologist, 30*, 583-594.

Pratt, C., Schmall, V., & Wright, S. (1987). Ethical concerns of family caregivers to dementia patients. *The Gerontologist, 27*, 632-638.

Pruchno, R. A. & Potashnik, S. I. (1989). Caregiving spouses: Physical and mental health in perspective. *Journal of the American Geriatric Society, 37,* 697-705.

Rose, J., & Del Maestro, S. (1990). Separation-individuation conflict as a model for understanding distressed caregivers: Psychodynamic and cognitive case studies. *The Gerontologist, 30,* 693-697.

Schulz, R., O'Brien, A. T., Bookwala, J. & Fleissner, R. (1995). Psychiatric and physical morbidity effects of dementia caregiving: prevalence, correlates, and causes. *The Gerontologist, 35,* 771-791.

Searle, M. S., & Mahon, M. J. (1991). Leisure education in a day hospital: The effects on selected social-psychological variables among older adults. *Canadian Journal of Community Mental Health, 10,* 95-109.

Szapocznik, J., Santisteban, D., Hervis, O. E., Spencer, F., & Kurtines, W. M. (1982). Life enhancement counseling and the treatment of depressed Cuban American elders. *Hispanic Journal of Behavioral Sciences, 4,* 487-502.

Thompson, E. H., Futterman, A. M., Gallagher-Thompson, D., Rose, J. M., & Lovett, S. B. (1993). Social support and caregiving burden in family caregivers of frail elders. *Journal of Gerontology, 48,* S245-S254.

Waldman, S. (1993). Surviving a fate worse than death: The plight of the homebound elderly. *Loss, Grief, and Care, 6,* 67-72.

Wheaton, B. (1985). Models for the stress-buffering functions of coping resources. *Journal of Health and Social Behavior, 26,* 352-364.

Zarit, S. H. & Zarit, J. M. (1982). Families under stress: Interventions for caregivers of senile dementia patients. *Pychotherapy: Theory, Research and Practice, 19* (4), 461-471.

Index

Page numbers followed by "f" indicate figures; page numbers followed by "t" indicate tables.

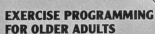